THE GLORY OF GOD AND THE
TRANSFIGURATION OF CHRIST

THE GLORY OF GOD AND THE TRANSFIGURATION OF CHRIST

by

ARTHUR MICHAEL RAMSEY
*Van Mildert Professor of Divinity in the University
of Durham and Canon of Durham Cathedral*

WIPF & STOCK · Eugene, Oregon

Wipf and Stock Publishers
199 W 8th Ave, Suite 3
Eugene, OR 97401

The Glory of God and the Transfiguration of Christ
By Ramsey, Arthur Michael
Copyright©1949 by Community of the Resurrection
ISBN 13: 978-1-60608-813-5
Publication date 6/8/2009
Previously published by Longmans, Green and Co., 1949

PREFACE

THE WORD 'glory' is often on the lips of Christian people, but they have sometimes only a vague idea as to its meaning. It is the purpose of this book to examine the conception of glory in the New Testament. Behind this conception there lies a fascinating piece of linguistic history, and within it are contained the greatest themes of Christian Theology. The word expresses in a remarkable way the unity of the doctrines of Creation, the Incarnation, the Cross, the Spirit, the Church and the world-to-come.

Akin to the doctrine of the glory of God is the event of the Transfiguration of Christ. To the first three evangelists the event had an importance far greater than its place in recent Biblical Theology or in Christian thought in the West generally would suggest. In the latter part of the book I have attempted to deal with some of the problems of the Transfiguration narratives and with the Theology of Transfiguration in the New Testament and in the later history of the Church. This Theology appears to me to have a special significance for the present time.

I hope that the bibliographies and references to other writers give some indication of my debt to them. I have especially to thank Mr. J. M. Wilkie, Lecturer in Theology in the University of Durham, for advice upon the Old Testament *prolegomena* which it was necessary to include in the work.

A. M. RAMSEY

Epiphany 1948.

'There's glory for you.' 'I don't know what you mean by glory,' Alice said. 'I meant "There's a nice knock-down argument for you".' 'But glory doesn't mean a nice knock-down argument,' Alice objected. 'When I use a word', Humpty Dumpty said in a rather scornful tone: 'it means just what I choose it to mean—neither more nor less.' CARROLL: Alice Through the Looking Glass.

'Glory is one of those words which we use in our common language with great latitude and haziness of meaning; and we sometimes carry our vagueness into the interpretation of Scripture: when Scripture has a precise and definite meaning, if we will only take the pains to ascertain it.' LIDDON: Christmastide in Saint Paul's.

'Can we rescue a word, and discover a universe? Can we study a language, and awake to the Truth? Can we bury ourselves in a lexicon, and arise in the presence of God?' HOSKYNS: Cambridge Sermons.

CONTENTS

THE GLORY OF GOD

I.	THE GLORY OF YAHVEH	page 9
II.	THE HISTORY OF A WORD	23
III.	THE GLORY IN THE RESURRECTION AND PAROUSIA	29
IV.	THE GLORY IN THE LIFE AND PASSION	36
V.	THE GLORY IN THE TEACHING OF SAINT PAUL	46
VI.	SAINT JOHN: THE PROLOGUE AND MINISTRY	53
VII.	SAINT JOHN: THE SUPPER AND PASSION	69
VIII.	THE GLORY AND THE CHRISTIAN FAITH	82
IX.	THE PRAISE OF HIS GLORY	91

THE TRANSFIGURATION OF CHRIST

X.	THE STUDY OF THE TRANSFIGURATION	101
XI.	THE TRANSFIGURATION IN SAINT MARK	112
XII.	THE TRANSFIGURATION IN OTHER NEW TESTAMENT WRITERS	120
XIII.	THE TRANSFIGURATION IN THE CHURCH	128
XIV.	THE GOSPEL OF TRANSFIGURATION	144

APPENDICES

i.	JESUS CHRIST, THE GLORY AND THE IMAGE	148
ii.	SOME ENGLISH COLLECTS	152
	SELECT BIBLIOGRAPHY	154
	INDEX	156

PART I: THE GLORY OF GOD

CHAPTER I

THE GLORY OF YAHVEH

THE WORD 'glory' in the English versions of the Old Testament is a translation of the Hebrew word *kabod*. Coming from a root which denotes 'heaviness' or 'weight' the word often means the 'riches' or the 'distinction' of a man or nation. Thus Laban's sons complain 'Jacob hath taken away all that was our father's; and of that which was our father's hath he gotten all the glory' (Gen. xxxi, 1). And the Psalmist gives the warning: 'Be not thou afraid when one is made rich, when the glory of his house is increased: for when he dieth he shall carry nothing away; His glory shall not descend after him' (Ps. xlix, 16-17). The *kabod* of a nation is its prosperity (cf. Isa. xvi, 14; xvii, 4; xxi, 16; lxi, 6); and, more than that, it is the distinction amid the world of nations which its prosperity expresses. Commenting on the word Israel Abrahams says: 'In English, the word *considerable* corresponds by its double use as to size and esteem.'[1]

A more personal use of the word also appears. *Kabod* can mean a man's self or spirit. The inward spirit of a man is his glory, the thing wherein his weight or worth is believed to consist. Sometimes the word is thus used with an intensity of feeling: 'Therefore my heart is glad, and my glory rejoiceth' (Ps. xvi, 9). 'My heart is fixed, O God; I will sing, yea, I will sing even with my glory' (Ps. cviii, 1). Jacob, denouncing the violence of his sons Simeon and Levi, cries: 'O my soul, come not into their council; unto their assembly, my glory, be not thou united' (Gen. xlix, 6). Perhaps the spirit is, in poetic speech, the glory of a man because it is his noblest part.[2]

---

[1] Abrahams: *The Glory of God*, p. 18.
[2] See Driver: *The Book of Genesis*, p. 383; Abrahams: op. cit., pp. 18-23; Pedersen: *Israel, its Life and Culture*, I-II, pp. 237-9. On the other hand it must be noticed that some scholars in the passages concerned read *kabed* or liver in place of *kabod*. In Gen. xlix, 6, this reading is supported by the LXX, τὰ ἥπατα μου.

GLORY AND TRANSFIGURATION

I

It is this word that is used to express the great theological conception that forms the subject of this book, the glory of God. If the conception is rich and complex in its final development this is no less true of its early history. *Kabod* denotes the revealed being or character of Yahveh, and also a physical phenomenon whereby Yahveh's presence is made known; and scholars have not been agreed as to the priority in time of one or other of these uses.

On the one hand it has been held that the root of the conception is the manifestation of Yahveh in the thunderstorm. This view was expounded in a thoroughgoing fashion by von Gall in his monograph *Die Herrlichkeit Gottes* (1900). He argued that the thunderstorm conception is apparent in all the pre-exilic references to the glory of Yahveh, including the vision of Isaiah in the temple; and he allowed only that variation in the conception began at the time of the exile: 'Ezekiel first separated the thunderstorm from the glory of Yahveh.' Eichrodt in his *Theologie des Alten Testaments* believes the thunderstorm idea to have priority, and says that those who think otherwise underrate the special importance of the Sinai traditions.[1] And the same view is taken by von Rad in the section which he contributed to the article on Δόξα in the *Theologisches Wörterbuch zum Neuen Testament*. 'God is, as the whole Old Testament testifies, invisible in Himself; but if He reveals Himself, or makes Himself known in meteorological appearances, we can with every right speak of "the glory of the LORD", an appearance which gives to men an impression of God's highest weight.'[2]

On the other hand there are scholars who have spoken with less decision, or have rejected the view which has just been described. G. B. Gray, in the article on *glory* in Hastings' Dictionary of the Bible, was unwilling to regard the thunderstorm theory of the origin of the doctrine as certain. Abrahams in *The Glory of God* (a sketch of the Biblical and Rabbinic teaching of singular beauty and piety) would not allow that there is in the Old Testament a local or meteorological conception of the *kabod* that is unconnected with the more 'inward' conception of the

[1] Eichrodt: op. cit., II, p. 9.   [2] *Theologisches Wörterbuch*, II, p. 241.

character and purpose of Yahveh. More recently, Helmud Kittel in *Die Herrlichkeit Gottes* (1934) has made a plea for the centrality and importance of the idea of Yahveh's *power* in connection with the *kabod*, while acknowledging that all chronological reconstructions of the history of the conception are precarious.

If the problem of origins has not been wholly solved we are not prevented from examining the content of the Biblical teaching, and that is the modest purpose of this book.

There can be no question that the presence of Yahveh was often connected with a storm of thunder and lightning. The imagery of thunder, lightning, fire, cloud, darkness recurs both in theophanies and in metaphorical descriptions of Yahveh's intervention in human affairs. The influence of the imagery seems to be far-reaching. The thunder is Yahveh's voice, the lightning is His arrows and spear; and it has been suggested that the cherubim and seraphim are creatures derived from the serpent-like lightning. We see the conception in the darkness, fire and smoke of Sinai, where volcanic imagery may also play its part. We see it also in the song of Deborah and Barak who tell of how the intervention of Yahveh in a storm brought victory to Israel. We see it above all in the brilliant storm-theophany of Psalm xviii. And in the storm-picture in Psalm xxix the word *kabod* significantly occurs:

> The voice of the LORD is upon the waters:
> The God of glory thundereth,
> Even the LORD upon the many waters.
> The voice of the LORD is powerful;
> The voice of the LORD is full of majesty.
> The voice of the LORD breaketh the cedars;
> Yea the LORD breaketh in pieces the cedars of Lebanon.
>
> (Ps. xxix, 3–5)

Abrahams, insistent as he is upon the inwardness of the doctrine of the *kabod*, traces to the storm-theophany all the varied imagery that came to be used for the divine presence, though ultimately only the light remained. 'The clouds are gone, the earthquake, the wind. Out of the primitive storm associations the only physical feature that endured was the illumination.'[1]

---
[1] *The Glory of God*, p. 56.

GLORY AND TRANSFIGURATION

Important however as is the storm-theophany, there are traces of another conception of the *kabod* in a pre-exilic *stratum* of the Pentateuch. In Exodus xxxiii, 12-23, the 'J writer' seems to be writing of a theophany of Yahveh in human form. First, Moses is told: 'My presence (Hebrew and LXX, *face*) will go with thee, and I will give thee rest.' Then, Moses is bold to ask: 'Shew me, I pray thee, thy glory,' and the answer comes that Moses must stand in a cleft of the rock while Yahveh passes by, and will then see only the back of Yahveh.[1] Perhaps the word *kabod* is here used to mitigate the anthropomorphism of the story. It seems that the importance of the passage lies in its suggestion that in pre-exilic times the storm-theophany was not the *only* known idea of the glory of Yahveh.

Sooner or later however the *kabod* appears in the Old Testament literature with the meaning of the character of Yahveh as revealed by His acts in history. There are a few passages in the Pentateuch where the *kabod* seems to suggest not the phenomena which indicate the presence of Yahveh so much as the *character* of Yahveh, made known to Israel by His mighty works as her deliverer and guide (Num. xiv, 22; Deut. v, 24). Here we touch the distinctive note of Israel's faith—the faith that Yahveh is not only a God who may be found in this or that locality or meteorological phenomenon, but also a God who has intervened in history to deliver Israel, made a covenant with her and revealed to her His stern moral demands and His righteous purpose. It is a faith that does not necessarily discard 'meteorology', but blends the meteorological and the ethical in its conception of God, as some of the Psalms were to shew:

> Clouds and darkness are round about him:
> Righteousness and darkness are the foundation of his throne.
> ... The heavens declare His righteousness,
> And all the peoples have seen his glory.
>
> (Ps. xcvii, 2-6)

It is above all in the prophets that this theology of the *kabod*

---

[1] Christian commentators have given highly spiritualized interpretations of this passage, e.g. Gregory of Nyssa, *Theol. Orat.* ii, 3, explains that though God is invisible men may yet see 'all the indications of Himself which He has left behind Him'.

THE GLORY OF YAHVEH

confronts us. Perhaps Isaiah of Jerusalem had a decisive influence upon it, as a result of his record of the vision which he saw in the temple.

> In the year that king Uzziah died I saw the Lord sitting upon a throne, high and lifted up, and his train filled the temple. Above him stood the seraphim: each one had six wings; with twain he covered his face, with twain he covered his feet, and with twain he did fly. And one cried unto another, and said, Holy, holy, holy, is the LORD of hosts: the whole earth is full of his glory. And the foundations of the thresholds were moved at the voice of him that cried, and the house was filled with smoke (Isa. vi, 1–4).

It is unlikely that this language can be dissociated from a quasi-physical conception. But the prophet's mind is at work on other levels than this. The glory of Yahveh is linked with His holiness; and if the holiness means a remoteness from all that is unrighteous, the glory is that union of sovereignty and righteousness which is the essence of the divine character. 'This holy, moral power, which is revealed to Isaiah in his vision is the Lord of the heavenly hosts, and the whole world reflects the lustre of his righteousness. History, human life is under the government of a righteous power that rules the world, and is not devoted merely to satisfying the unethical desires of a petty nation or tolerating its sins.'[1] Isaiah's words have a significance for the revelation of the glory of God that reaches far beyond the Old Testament into the worship of the Christian Church. In the liturgy of the Church the adoration of the divine glory in the words of the song of the seraphim immediately precedes the eucharistic action in which the glory of the Cross of Christ is set forth.

The second Isaiah, the prophet of the exile, went further than his predecessor. He made explicit the monotheism which the first Isaiah implied, and proclaimed a God who is incomparable, the Lord of history, the only God, the first and the last, the potential Saviour of all the nations. Writing on the eve of the great deliverance which enabled the exiles to return to Jerusalem he sees this deliverance as a drama in which the glory of Yahveh is disclosed.

[1] G. B. Gray: *Isaiah*, International Critical Commentary, pp. 106–7.

GLORY AND TRANSFIGURATION

> Every valley shall be exalted, and every mountain and hill shall be made low: and the crooked shall be made straight, and the rough places plain: and the glory of the LORD shall be revealed, and all flesh shall see it together, for the mouth of the LORD hath spoken it.
> (Isa. xl, 4-5)

Yahveh will not 'give his glory to another' (xlii, 8, xlviii, 11), and His people are those who are 'called by my name, and whom I have created for my glory' (xliii, 7).

Finally, the post-exilic writer of Isaiah lx, pictures Jerusalem as the scene of the shining-forth of the glory of Yahveh to the nations.

> Arise, shine: for thy light is come, and the glory of the LORD is risen upon thee. For, behold, darkness shall cover the earth, and gross darkness the peoples: but the LORD shall arise upon thee and his glory shall be seen upon thee. And nations shall come to thy light, and kings to the brightness of thy rising (Isa. lx, 1-3).

Here the idea of radiance has the greatest prominence. Indeed, in the *kabod* of Yahveh radiance, power and righteous character are inextricably blended; and the word thus tells of a theology in which the attributes of God in Himself are inseparable from His attractiveness and saving activity in the world. Israel's knowledge of God's glory has its corollary in Israel's obligation to reflect God's character. If, for instance, she cares for the poor and the naked, she has the promise:

> Then shall thy light break forth as the morning, and thy healing shall go forth speedily; and thy righteousness shall go before thee; the glory of the LORD shall be thy rearward (Isa. lviii, 8).

The Psalmists tell a similar tale. But to a greater extent they use the word in connection with the *future* manifestation of the glory and the recognition of the glory by the nations. Yahveh is the 'king of glory' (Ps. xxiv, 7-10),[1] and the acknowledgment of this in all the world will be the consummation of His purpose.

---

[1] We could have a closer understanding of the Psalter if we knew more about the liturgical occasions upon which the Psalms were used. Mowinckel put forward the theory that there was in pre-exilic Israel an annual New-Year Festival of the enthroning of Yahveh, borrowed from the Babylonian ceremony of the enthroning of the deity Marduk; and he connects a number of the Psalms with

THE GLORY OF YAHVEH

Declare His glory among the nations:
His marvellous works among all the peoples.
(Ps. xcvi, 3)
Be thou exalted O God, above the heavens;
Let thy glory be over all the earth.
(Ps. lvii, 11)
Surely his salvation is nigh them that fear him;
That glory may dwell in our land.
Mercy and truth are met together;
Righteousness and peace have kissed each other.
(Ps. lxxxv, 9–10)

Thus the Psalmists, unite with the prophets in using the word glory to tell of Yahveh's universal sovereignty and its future vindication.

2

When all this has been said only the half has been told about the doctrine of the *kabod*, for there is also the special conception that appears in the exilic and post-exilic writings of the Priestly School. Here the *kabod* is connected with a local theophany on mount Sinai or in the tabernacle and the temple. It is a physical phenomenon, manifest to ordinary vision. At the same time it has to be remembered that this 'localized' conception is held in tension with a deepened conviction that Yahveh is transcendent and never to be confined to any earthly dwelling.

In the fashioning of this conception it seems that Ezekiel, the prophet of the earlier years of the Babylonian exile, had a big influence. Though he is familiar with the idea of the *kabod* as the

---

this festival. It is easy to see the appropriateness of some of the Psalms for this ceremony (cf. Ps. xxiv, 7, 'Lift up your heads, o ye gates, and the King of glory shall come in'), and Mowinkel would translate 'The Lord reigneth' (Ps. xciii, 1; xcvii, 1) as 'Yahveh has become king'. There is however no clear evidence that this annual festival ever existed. And we have recently had a reminder that it is a mistake to attach too much importance to the primitive significance of Israel's cults if we are trying to assess the meaning of Israel's developed faith and theology, so that it would seem highly precarious to seek in Mowinckel's theory a clue to the Biblical doctrine of the glory of God. Cf. H. H. Rowley: *The Rediscovery of the Old Testament*, pp. 125–7. The theory is criticised by N. Snaith in *The Jewish New Year Festival*, 1948.

15

GLORY AND TRANSFIGURATION

divine character (cf. Ezek. xxxix, 21) he uses the word almost always of a fiery appearance descried in his own visions. It is bright as a rainbow (i, 28, x, 4), it moves (ix, 3, x, 4, xliii, 2), it is borne upon cherubim (x, 19, xi, 22), it is accompanied by the sound of a great rushing (iii, 12). In his opening vision by the banks of the river Chebar Ezekiel, amid the dazzling phenomena of the storm-cloud, the four living creatures, the chariot and the appearance of a man, saw the fiery brightness which was 'the appearance of the likeness of the glory of the LORD'. And he fell upon his face, awestruck at the transcendent and omnipresent God who makes His presence known to exiles in Babylonia no less than to the people in Jerusalem. In subsequent visions he tells of the glory of the LORD leaving the city of Jerusalem when it is doomed to destruction. Borne by cherubim upon a chariot the glory moves forth from the threshold of the house and stands upon the mountain to the east of the city (x, 18–24; xi, 22 ff). But restoration will come. Ezekiel's theodicy leads on from the judgment upon Jerusalem, through the discipline of the exile, to the prediction of a new heart and a new spirit and a restored community. This community will be ruled by the priests and will have the temple-worship as its centre. The prophet sees in vision the glory of the LORD returning to the temple, the same appearance of the glory which he had seen by the river Chebar (xliii, 1–5). The name of the city is 'Yahveh is there' (xlviii, 35).

It is only in visions that the phenomenon of the glory is described as occurring. He does not speak of it as something which his contemporaries see with the naked eye. On the other hand the Priestly Writer speaks of the *kabod* as a phenomenon which the ordinary human eyes of all the people can see. This is the phenomenon which he describes in his narratives of the wilderness, of Sinai and the tabernacle.

The Priestly Writer tells of the Mosaic period in the wilderness so as to make his narrative reflect the belief and institutions of himself and his school in the post-exilic period. But he builds upon earlier traditions. In the J document Yahveh moves before the children of Israel in a cloud (Exod. xiv, 19–24). In the E document on the other hand the cloud does not move as a guide: it comes from time to time and stands at the door of the tent of meeting (Exod. xxxiii, 9–10). The Priestly writer has his own

THE GLORY OF YAHVEH

conception. The cloud appears at Sinai. It is seen in the camp only when the tabernacle has been completed. It dwells continually in the tabernacle. By day it is seen as a cloud, by night as a fiery pillar. If it should be seen to be fiery by day, there unmistakably is the *kabod*. The cloud is not itself the glory, nor is it part of a set of storm-phenomena which constitute the glory. Rather is it a covering which conceals the glory that shines through it from within.[1] At Sinai the first appearance took place.

> And the glory of the LORD abode upon Mount Sinai, and the cloud covered it six days; and the seventh day he called unto Moses out of the midst of the cloud. And the appearance of the glory of the LORD was like devouring fire on the top of the mount in the eyes of the children of Israel (Exod. xxiv, 16-17).

Moses entered the cloud, and went up onto the mount, and there remained forty days and forty nights. And when he descended the skin of his face shone and he put a veil over it to conceal it from the people while he spoke with them (Exod. xxxiv, 29-35).

The conception of the *kabod* which we find in these narratives of the wilderness appears also in the descriptions of the temple of Solomon. In 1 Kings viii, 10, after the ark was brought into the temple 'the cloud filled the house of the LORD, so that the priests could not stand to minister by reason of the cloud: for the glory of the LORD filled the house of the LORD.'[2] The description recurs in 2 Chronicles vii, 1-3. The story reflects the tension which runs through the religion of post-exilic Judaism, the tension between the transcendence of Yahveh and the presence in the temple. He dwells in the temple, yet He is the creator of the world; and the 'thick darkness' of which Solomon speaks 'symbolizes the mystery of divinity, the contrast between His nearness to Israel and His essential power and majesty'.[3]

This tension is part and parcel of the religion of post-exilic

[1] Cf. von Rad: 'Hier ist der *Kabod* keine Wettererscheinung—die Wolke ist ja gar nicht Teil des *Kabod*, sondern nur Hülle—vielmehr ein reales In-Erscheinung-Treten der Herrlichkeit Gottes.'

[2] Von Rad suggests that this passage may reflect not the proper priestly conception of the *kabod* hidden within the cloud, but an earlier doctrine of the cloud itself as the *kabod*. *Theologisches Wörterbuch*, II, p. 243.

[3] J. Skinner: *The Book of Kings*, Century Bible, ad. loc.

GLORY AND TRANSFIGURATION

Judaism, whose form and spirit are expressed in the priestly narratives about the tabernacle and the temple. It was the religion whose centre was the temple built by Zerubbabel. Its motive was the consecration of the life of the community to Yahveh, its first activity was the sacrificial cultus, its longing was for the presence of Yahveh in the midst. But the intensifying of the local importance of the temple went hand in hand with the deepening of the sense of awe and guilt before 'the high and lofty One that inhabiteth eternity, whose name is Holy' (Isa. lvii, 15). Hence it is significant that the post-exilic literature, while it dwells upon the presence of the glory in the ancient tabernacle, nowhere speaks of the glory as present in the *contemporary* post-exilic temple. The priestly theology lacked a note of confidence. The longings of Israel were not satisfied. The fulfilment of the exilic prophecies had not been completed; and these prophecies became more and more projected into the future. But the hope remains; and one day Israel will have the vision of the *kabod* of her God, whether by His dwelling with man upon the stage of history or by the coming of a new heaven and a new earth bathed in the light of the divine radiance.

3

We pass now beyond the books of the Hebrew Canon of the Old Testament, and find two developments in late pre-Christian Judaism which are of great importance.

The first is the conception of the *Shekinah*. The growing sense of the divine transcendence caused the Hebrew mind to shrink from references to the direct intervention of Yahveh in human affairs. Hence in the Targums, or rabbinic paraphrases of Scripture, certain Aramaic words were used as 'buffers' to enable the divine intervention to be described without the language of direct description. Among these words are *Memra*, connected with the *word*; *Yekara*, connected with the *glory*; *Shekinah*, connected with the *dwelling*. Of these words the *Shekinah* is the most prominent in connection with the theme of this book.

Some illustrations will shew the use of this word by the Targumists.

THE GLORY OF YAHVEH

Hebrew text	Targum
Lev. xxvi, 12: I will walk among you.	I will cause my Shekinah to dwell among you.
Exod. xxv, 8: . . . that I may dwell in your midst.	. . . that I may cause my Shekinah to dwell in your midst.
Isa. lvii, 17: I hid myself.	I caused my Shekinah to depart.

Whenever the text of Scripture seemed to impose limitations of space upon God the Targumists were wont to introduce the Shekinah. To avoid saying that God dwelt or God came or even that God was in heaven this new conception was employed.

The Shekinah is not the glory. Once only in the Targums is the word used as a translation of *kabod* (Zech. ii, 9); and in many passages Shekinah and glory are clearly distinguished, as when the Targum of Leviticus xxvi, 12, says: 'I will place the glory of my Shekinah among you.' Nor is the Shekinah a personal or hypostatic intermediary with attributes and functions. Rather is it a way of speaking about God such as conveys the truth of His omnipresence, accessibility and special activity within the created world without infringing the doctrine of His transcendence. Rabbi Jose ben Halafta says: 'Never did the Shekinah descend to earth, nor did Moses and Elijah ascend to heaven; for it is written, the heavens are the Lord's and the earth he has given to the children of men.' On another occasion a caviller asks: 'How many Shekinahs are there?' and the answer is: 'How does the sun get into that man's house?'

It is possible that in the Midrash and the Talmud the Shekinah is regarded more as an intermediary with functions than in the Targums.[1] Some resemblance to the conceptions of the Wisdom or the Spirit is suggested for instance by the saying in *Pirke Aboth*: 'Two that sit together and are occupied in the words of the law have the Shekinah among them.' But the idea of the Shekinah expresses the Jewish conception of the divine in a way

---

[1] G. F. Moore in *Harvard Theological Review*, XXV, pp. 41-8 ('Intermediaries in Jewish Theology'), protests against a tendency of Christian theologians to treat Shekinah and Memra as if they were metaphysical hypostases akin to the Christian doctrine of the Logos. But his view that the terms are *mere* 'buffer-words' is in turn criticized by R. D. Middleton in *Jewish Quarterly Review*, XXIX, pp. 101-3. ('Logos and Shekinah in the Fourth Gospel.')

that easily eludes exact understanding on the part of a non-Jew. 'The conception made God as near to every worshipper as any modern man could desire. To the first century is attributed the explanation why God revealed Himself in the lonely thorn bush. It was to teach that no spot upon the earth is empty of the Shekinah. Yet it was finely perceived that God is in one sense only 'near' when His creatures are present, and ready to apprehend His nearness. It is they who for practical purposes turn His transcendence into immanence. Hence the doctrine that virtue, Israel, the sanctuary and the Law, all bring down God or the Shekinah from heaven to earth, while sin and idolatry remove him. Yet the divine nearness realized by the Israelite through the Law did not interfere with the theoretic apprehension that God was not, like a human person, limited by any particular place.'[1]

The differences therefore between the rabbinic conception of the Shekinah and the Biblical conception of the *kabod* are as significant as the resemblances. But we shall see how these and other differences come to be fused in the language and doctrine of the Septuagint. The word δόξα represented both *kabod* and Shekinah; and the word σκηνή represented both tabernacle and Shekinah. Hence conceptions which are distinct in Hebrew and Aramaic literature became, in the Septuagint, fused into a unified imagery of God's glory and God's dwelling or tabernacling with His people. This unified imagery is the background of much of the thought of the writers of the New Testament.

The other late development is the imagery of the messianic glory particularly in the Apocalyptic books. Glory is an attribute of the Messiah, of the righteous in the messianic age and sometimes of heaven and earth themselves when they shall be drenched in the light of the divine radiance.

The Book of Enoch has much to say about the messianic glory. The visions often refer to 'the glory', 'the Lord of glory', 'the throne of glory'. The writer tells of a vision of heaven in which there is a manifestation of glory akin to Exodus or Ezekiel.

> And from underneath the throne came streams of flaming fire so that I could not look thereon. And the Great Glory sat theron, and

[1] C. G. Montefiore in *The Beginnings of Christianity*, vol. I, pp. 38-9.

THE GLORY OF YAHVEH

His raiment shone more brightly than the sun and was whiter than any snow. None of the angels could enter and behold His face by reason of the magnificence and glory, and no flesh could behold him.
(Enoch xiv, 19-21)

In visions of the final judgment the Messiah will sit upon 'the throne of glory' (xlvii, 3; lv, 4; lx, 8; lxi, 2; lxii, 2, 5; lxix, 27-29), and the righteous shall be clothed in garments of glory (lxii, 16); the light will shine upon their faces (xxxviii, 4), and they will be in the light of the sun (lviii, 3). Other Apocalyptic books contain the same ideas: the righteous will both see the divine glory and reflect it. They will 'adore the glory of the Most High' (4 Ezra vii, 78); and they will 'be changed into every form they desire, from beauty into loveliness, and from light into the splendour of glory' (2 Baruch li, 8-10). The visions of the future vary as between earth and heaven. Sometimes the scene of blazing light is set in heaven; sometimes Jerusalem on earth is enveloped in light (2 Baruch v, 1-5).

Nor is it only in the Apocalyptic writers that the hope of the messianic glory is entertained. The Pharisaic expectation of a messianic king finds classic expression in the Psalms of Solomon, and here we read of the reign of the Messiah in Israel when the nations will see his glory and the glory of the Lord (Ps. Sol. xvii, 34). A special interest (in view of the latter part of this book) belongs to an episode in the Second Book of Maccabees. Jeremiah conceals the tabernacle and the ark in a chamber in the rock, where they will remain hidden,

> until God gather the people together again, and mercy come: and then shall the LORD disclose these things, and the glory of the LORD shall be seen, and the cloud (2 Macc. ii, 7-8).

4

Such is the unity in diversity of the doctrine of the glory of God in Israel. There is a unity because from very early times the conception of the *kabod* was linked with Israel's faith in a righteous and sovereign God. There is a diversity because the faith of Israel did not drop in a neat pattern from heaven but was wrought out in the ups and downs of a turbulent history. No-

GLORY AND TRANSFIGURATION

where are the tensions of Biblical theology greater than in the doctrine of the glory. It speaks on the one hand of an invisible and omnipresent God and on the other hand of a meteorological phenomenon; on the one hand of Israel's transcendent king and judge and on the other hand of a presence tabernacling in Israel's midst. But in these tensions the validity of the theology of the Old Testament lies. 'Am I a God at hand, saith the LORD, and not a God afar off?' (Jer. xxiii, 23). Always in tension these contrasted aspects of the divine glory find their true unity when the Word by whom all things were made became flesh and dwelt among us, and the glory of Bethlehem and Calvary is the glory of the eternal God.

CHAPTER II

THE HISTORY OF A WORD

1

THE MAKERS of the Septuagint, that is the Greek version of the Old Testament written in Alexandria, were faced with the need for a Greek word to translate the Hebrew *kabod*; and they used the word δόξα. By so using it they gave it a sense totally different from its original meaning in Greek literature. No word in the Bible has a more fascinating history. That a word which meant human opinion or human reputation should come to express the greatest theological ideas both of the Old Testament and of the New is one of the most signal instances of the impact of theology upon language.

In Greek literature the word δόξα has two familiar meanings. With its roots in the verb δοκέω, 'to think' or 'to seem', it means *opinion* and also *distinction* or *fame*—what a man himself thinks, and what other people think about him. The Latin *opinio* and *gloria* serve well to express the two uses. There is no evidence for thinking that the word is originally connected with light or radiance.[1]

2

So far the familiar Greek uses. But with the Septuagint a revolution of language occurs. The authors of the Greek Bible aban-

---

[1] Kittel analyses the normal meaning of δόξα thus: 'a. von "ich meine": die Meinung die ich habe (opinio); b. von "ich gelte": die Geltung, die Meinung, die man über mich hat (gloria).' T.W., II, p. 237. Kittel however also follows Bechtel, *Die attische Frauennamen nach ihrem Systeme dargestellt*, in thinking that *one* instance can be found of a connection between δόξα and light, namely in its use as a name for women or ships as one of a number of *Lichtname* such as Φέγγος, Ἀστήρ, Φωσφόρος, Σελήνη. On the other hand, Kittel's namesake, Helmud Kittel, in *Die Herrlichkeit Gottes*, pp. 24-7, suggests the possibility that Δόξα when used as a proper name belongs not to the *Lichtname* class but to a *Ruhmvolle* class with such names as Ἀρετή, Κλέω, Εὐφημία, Ἐλευθερία.

23

GLORY AND TRANSFIGURATION

don one of the familiar uses—δόξα in the sense of opinion: at the very most two instances of this use can be cited and one of these is doubtful. They retain the other familiar use—δόξα in the sense of men's honour or distinction: Joseph had his glory in Egypt, Simon Maccabaeus had his kingly glory. But by far the most frequent use of δόξα in the Septuagint is as a translation of the *kabod* of Yahveh, both in the sense of His character and might and in the sense of the radiance of His presence. Δόξα is above all else the glory of God, and the Greek word has found an employment far removed from its original human and man-centred connotation. Yahveh is ὁ θεὸς τῆς δόξης (Ps. xxviii, 3), and ὁ βασιλεὺς τῆς δόξης (Ps. xxiii, 7).

More still, while δόξα is used to translate *kabod* and to acquire those meanings which the word *kabod* covers, it is also used to translate other Hebrew words of kindred meaning, words which we render 'majesty', 'beauty', 'excellency', and the like. As a result of this wide use the δόξα of God is more prominent in the Septuagint than is the *kabod* of God in the Hebrew Bible, and the doctrine of the divine glory is presented with a greater unity and impressiveness.[1] And a still wider use is to be recorded. Flexible in its ability to express every aspect of the divine *kabod* and every Hebrew word akin to the *kabod*, δόξα served also to translate the Aramaic Shekinah. Thus it was that the two conceptions, *kabod* and *Shekinah*, which are properly separate in meaning as in language, came to be fused together by Greek-speaking Jews. Indeed the Greek word proved itself to be in a striking way both servant and master. Submitting itself to the service of a Hebrew theology it presses a variety of Hebrew words and ideas into the unity of its own new and massive conception.[2]

---

[1] Δόξα is used in the LXX to translate these words: *osher*, riches, Gen. xxxi, 16; *gā'ōn*, majesty, excellency, Isa. xiv, 11; xxiv, 14; Exod. xv, 7; *hod*, honour, Num. xxvii, 20, majesty, Job xxxvii, 22; *tiph'arah*, beauty, 2 Chron. iii, 6; *ōz*, strength, Ps. lxviii, 34, Isa. xii, 2; *hon*, wealth, Ps. cxii, 3; *gē-ûth*, majesty, Isa. xxvi, 10; *yŏphi*, beauty, Isa. xxxiii, 17; *on*, might, Isa. xl, 26; *hadar*, comeliness, Isa. liii, 2; *pĕ'ēr*, garland, Isa. lxi, 3; *yamin*, right hand, Ps. lxiii, 8; *tehillah*, praises, Exod. xv, 11; *tō'ar*, form, Isa. lii, 14.

[2] How the word δόξα came to be used in the LXX in this totally new sense is discussed, inconclusively, by H. Kittel, op. cit., pp. 59-68. He suggests that the glory of God is a conception which partly overlaps the ideas of the *honour* of God (Ehre) and the *fame* of God (Ruhm), and that these 'secular' conceptions

THE HISTORY OF A WORD

Some illustrations of δόξα, where it occurs in the Septuagint without any corresponding mention of 'glory' in the Hebrew, may shew how impressive the idea has become in the thought and language of Greek-speaking Jews:

Exod. xv, 11	*glorified* in his saints, marvellous in his *glories*, doing wonders.
Exod. xxxiii, 19	I will pass by thee in *my glory*.
2 Chron. ii, 6	The heaven and the heaven of heavens cannot contain *his glory*.
Isa. xxxiii, 17	Ye shall see the king in *his glory*.
Isa. lii, 1	Put on *thy glory*, O Jerusalem.
Isa. lii, 13	Behold my servant shall learn wisdom and shall be lifted up and exceedingly *glorified*.
Isa. liii, 2	He hath neither form nor *glory*.

Akin to the use of δόξα in the Septuagint is the use of σκηνή and κατασκηνοῦν, the noun and the verb for 'tabernacle'. These words appear to fuse together into a doctrinal unity certain ideas of the Scriptures and the Targums. The word *shaken* often occurs in the Hebrew Bible to signify the dwelling of Yahveh with His people. And now, in the Septuagint, κατασκηνοῦν does duty for *shaken* while σκηνή does duty both for the Shekinah and for the tabernacle or tent of meeting. Hence there comes a blending of the imagery of the tent of meeting and the imagery of Yahveh dwelling with His people within a single unified conception of 'tabernacling'.

Num. xxxv, 34	For I am the LORD tabernacling (κατασκηνῶν) in the midst of the sons of Israel.
Ps. lxxxiv, 10	His salvation is nigh them that fear him, that glory may dwell (κατασκηνῶσαι) in our land.
Zech. ii, 10	Rejoice and be glad, daughter of Zion, for behold I come and I will dwell (κατασκηνώσω) in the midst of thee, saith the LORD.
Ecclus. xxiv, 8	(God addresses Wisdom.) Dwell (κατασκήνωσον) in Jacob, and have thine inheritance in Israel.

provide a groundwork of language for the Biblical conception. Evidence for the Jewish use of δόξα in its new sense having an influence upon Greek magical writing in the papyri at a later date is given by W. L. Knox: *Some Hellenistic Elements in the New Testament*, p. 85.

GLORY AND TRANSFIGURATION

Thus the Septuagint sets the imagery of glory, tabernacle and the dwelling of Yahveh in a composite pattern. This pattern was familiar to the Greek-speaking Jews of the time of the apostles, and it lay to hand (as we shall see) for the Christian Church to use and to build upon.

It is not however only the theological meaning which we find in the Septuagint. Side by side with the theological meaning, there remains the use of δόξα for man's honour and distinction. So we get passages in which the glory of man and the glory of God jostle side by side, indicating the conflict which is one of the great issues of the Bible. It is not only that men in crude unbelief set the pride of human glory in rebellion against God: it is also that they twist their God-given privileges into a means of human self-glorification. Some of the later books give a glimpse of the problem. Thus in Ecclesiasticus we read:

> Let us now praise famous men, and our fathers that begat us. The LORD manifested in them great glory.
> (Ecclus. xliv, 1-2)

It is God's glory, in the strictest sense His alone. But it is also *their* glory for

> Their seed shall remain for ever,
> And their glory shall not be blotted out (xliv, 13).

Hence the tension. There is the glory of God, and the glory of those things which He has instituted; and the writer says of Simon the great high-priest:

> How glorious was he when the people gathered round him at his coming forth from the sanctuary (l, 5).

Similarly 1 Maccabees tells of the glory of Israel, despoiled by the foreign tyrant and fought for by God's loyal people, and of the glory of Simon Maccabaeus in the prowess of his conquests. The issue is plain. God gives glory to men, as when for instance He gave Joseph 'eternal glory' (Wisd. x, 14); but the glory is from Him, and only the recollection that it is from Him will save men from the glory which they heap upon themselves. The final diagnosis of the conflict between glory true and glory false comes in the words of our Lord in the Fourth Gospel:

THE HISTORY OF A WORD

How can ye believe, which receive glory one of another, and the glory that cometh from the only God ye seek not? (John v, 44).

3

We are led thus to the δόξα of the New Testament, which forms the subject of the remainder of this book.

No instance occurs in the New Testament of δόξα meaning 'opinion'. This use has disappeared as decisively as in the Septuagint.

There are instances of δόξα meaning, as in classical Greek literature, human distinction or honour. So we read of the glory of the kingdoms of this world (Matt. iv, 8), of Solomon in all his glory (Matt. vi, 29), of the refusal of the apostles to seek glory of men (1 Thess. ii, 6) and of 'glories' in the sense of 'dignities' (Jude 8; 2 Pet. ii, 10). In 1 Peter i, 11, the glories that follow the Passion of Christ are probably 'triumphs', as in Exodus xxxiii, 5.[1] Elsewhere we find the word in the sense of good repute or renown (2 Cor. vi, 8; 1 Thess. ii, 6) or that which brings good repute or renown (1 Thess. ii, 20; 2 Cor. viii, 23; Rev. xxi, 24, 26). In 1 Corinthians xi, 7, 'the woman is the glory of the man', the use of δόξα is paralleled in an inscription where a wife is described as her husband's glory.[2]

These 'non-theological' uses of δόξα form however but a tiny fraction of the occurrences of the word in the New Testament. The field is dominated by uses drawn from the Old Testament doctrine of the *kabod* and transformed by the revelation of the divine glory in the events of the Gospel.

Within this theological use in the New Testament it is sometimes the idea of light and radiance that is prominent. Both in the sayings of Jesus about the future Parousia, and in the teaching of the apostles about the heavenly state of Jesus and the future destiny of the Christians, δόξα describes a celestial brightness and splendour. Sometimes on the other hand the emphasis of the word is upon the character or power of God, and the phrase 'the riches of his glory' (Eph. i, 18) is a reminder of the Biblical

[1] Cf. Selwyn: *The First Epistle of Saint Peter*, ad. loc.
[2] ἡ δόξα Σωφρονίου Δουκίλλα εὐλογημένη, quoted by Lietzmann *An die Korinther*, ad. loc.

roots of the doctrine. It seems that references to the rabbinic idea of the Shekinah are, despite the indiscriminate language used by some modern writers, infrequent. The apostles pierce through the later Jewish developments to the *Biblical* ideas of the glory, and find these ideas coming to rest in the revelation of God in Jesus Christ.

It is often hard to determine which aspect of the glory is present in a particular passage, and indeed the different aspects melt into one another in the New Testament as in the Old. But in every aspect of the glory the person of Jesus Christ becomes the dominant fact. In so far as δόξα means the power and character of God, the key to that power and character is found in what God has done in the events of the Gospel. In so far as δόξα is the divine splendour, Jesus Christ *is* that splendour. And in so far as a state of light and radiance awaits the Christian as his final destiny, that light and radiance draw their meaning from the presence and person of Christ. Hence new possibilities of language emerge: such is the place of Jesus Christ in relation to the divine glory that it is possible to speak of *the glory of Christ*, and by those words to mean no less than the glory of God Himself.

It follows that the word δόξα both reflects and expresses the pattern of the apostolic faith. This faith has as its groundwork the glory of God in creation, in nature and in the history of Israel; it has as its centre the glory of God in the birth, life, death and exaltation of Jesus, and as its goal the participation of mankind and of all creation in the eschatological glory of the Messiah. Creation, redemption, eschatology form a single pattern; and to separate them is to render each of them unintelligible and to distort the theology of the apostolic age.

CHAPTER III

THE GLORY IN THE RESURRECTION AND THE PAROUSIA

IF THE greater final significance belongs to those uses of δόξα in the New Testament which connect it with the character and power of God revealed in the Gospel, there can be no question of the greater prominence of those uses which connect it with light and radiance. In the Synoptic Gospels, in the Acts of the Apostles, in Saint Paul's Epistles and in the Petrine writings it denotes the radiant, heavenly state into which our Lord was exalted at the Resurrection and Ascension and into which the Christians hope to enter at His Parousia. This eschatological use seems to be the groundwork of the apostolic doctrine.

I

In the sayings recorded in the Synoptic Gospels our Lord uses the word 'glory', apart from a few instances of a 'secular' use,[1] solely in connection with the future. The imagery is akin to that familiar in the Apocalyptic books; but, if in one or two passages there is a similarity to the language of the Similitudes of Enoch (e.g. Matt. xxv, 31), the influence of the description of the Son of Man in Daniel vii is more prominent.

> For whosoever shall be ashamed of me and of my words in this adulterous and sinful generation, the Son of Man shall be ashamed of him, when he cometh in the glory of his Father with the holy angels.
> (Mark viii, 38)
> And then shall they see the Son of Man coming in the clouds with great power and glory (Mark xiii, 26).
> But when the Son of Man shall come in his glory, and all the angels with him, then shall he sit on the throne of his glory.
> (Matt. xxv, 31)

[1] See p. 27.

GLORY AND TRANSFIGURATION

Verily I say unto you, that ye which have followed me, in the regeneration when the Son of Man shall sit on the throne of his glory, ye also shall sit upon twelve thrones, judging the twelve tribes of Israel (Matt. xix, 28).

The request of the sons of Zebedee contains the word δόξα in a similar sense:

Grant unto us that we may sit, one on thy right hand and the other on thy left hand in thy glory (Mark x, 37).

The glory lies in the future, beyond the Passion.[1]

The picture of the Son of Man in glory is no novelty. In Daniel vii the Son of Man coming on the clouds of heaven is a symbol in vision of the people of the saints of the most High receiving sovereignty after the destruction of the series of world empires. In the Similitudes of Enoch 'that Son of Man' seems to be a heavenly Messiah who comes to reign and to judge. In Psalm viii the Son of Man means mankind, and he is crowned with 'glory and honour' as God's vicegerent over the created world. Scholars are divided as to the primary element in the background to our Lord's use of the title. Yet the *novel* element in our Lord's use of it is unmistakable: 'the Son of Man must suffer.' It is by a road of suffering that Jesus must enter into the glory which the Father has in store for Him as Messiah, King and Judge. He is *barnasha*, 'the Man'—the Man through whose heavenly glory and preceding suffering the Kingdom of God comes. In the latter part of Saint Mark's Gospel the sayings of Jesus disclose the twofold picture (1) the Son of Man suffering, (2) the Son of Man in glory.[2] And side by side with this theme there is the challenge to the disciples: if they will suffer, they too will share in the glory.

---

[1] It is interesting to notice a connection between δόξα and δύναμις, Mark viii, 38-ix, 1; xiii, 26; and a connection between δόξα and βασιλεία, Mark viii, 38-ix, 1; Mark x, 37. cf. Matt. xx, 21; 1 Thess. ii, 12; 'who calleth you into his own kingdom and glory.' Cf. Ps. cxlv, 11: 'They shall speak of the glory of thy kingdom, and talk of thy power.'

[2] The texts relating to the Son of Man in glory are commonly taken to refer to a *return* in glory to judge the world. The possibility cannot be excluded that the emphasis is rather, as in Dan. vii, upon an *entrance* into the glory associated with the clouds of heaven. Cf. W. K. Lowther-Clarke's essay on 'The Clouds of Heaven' in his book *Divine Humanity*.

THE GLORY IN THE RESURRECTION AND PAROUSIA

2

The eschatological use of the word 'glory' is renewed in the teaching of the apostolic Church, but meanwhile the event of the Resurrection has wrought a decisive change. Jesus has been exalted into the radiant light of heavenly glory; and in the conviction of His Lordship, as risen from the dead and now in heaven, the apostles await with certainty His coming to receive His followers into glory with Him.

The glory is frequently linked with the Resurrection and the Ascension.

God ... hath glorified his servant Jesus, whom ye delivered up.
(Acts iii, 13)
But he (Stephen) ... looked up stedfastly into heaven, and saw the glory of God, and Jesus standing on the right hand of God.
(Acts vii, 55)
Christ was raised from the dead through the glory of the Father.
(Rom. vi, 4)
God which raised him from the dead, and gave him glory.
(1 Peter i, 21)
He who was manifested in the flesh, justified in the spirit, seen of angels, preached among the nations, believed on in the world, received up in glory. (1 Tim. iii, 16.)

The wide diffusion of these passages amongst the apostolic writings (including one quasi-credal passage) shows how fundamental is the belief that the Resurrection was *into glory*. But in these passages the word 'glory' has more than one relation to the event. By the power of the Father's glory the Resurrection of Christ was wrought (Rom. vi, 4).[1] Glory was conferred upon Christ by the Father through the exaltation (Acts iii, 13; 1 Pet. i, 21). And into the radiance of the glory Christ was exalted (Acts vii, 55; 1 Tim iii, 16). It may be that this last conception owed something to the vision of Saint Paul at his conversion, when he 'saw on the way a light from heaven, above the brightness of

---

[1] This is assuming that δόξα in Rom. vi, 4, is akin to κράτος in meaning, cf. Ps. Sol. xi, 9, ἀναστῆσαι κύριος τὸν Ἰσραὴλ ἐν ὀνόματι τῆς δόξης αὐτοῦ. But it has been suggested that Saint Paul is thinking here of the radiance of the Shekinah piercing the gloom of Sheol, an idea found amongst the Rabbis, cf. *Bereshith Rabba, Gen*, xliv, 8.

GLORY AND TRANSFIGURATION

the sun' (Acts xxvi, 13; cf. ix, 3; xxii, 6; 2 Cor. iv, 6). The risen Christ is now in 'the body of his glory' (Phil. iii, 21). But there is no reason to suppose that the apostolic belief in Christ's heavenly glory *originated* from Saint Paul's vision, for the conviction that Jesus was now in glory would be an inevitable corollary of the primitive conviction that, raised from death and exalted to heaven, He was 'at the right hand of God'.

For a while 'the heavens must receive him' (cf. Acts iii, 21), but at the Parousia the glory which is now hidden will be unveiled, and the faithful will see it and share in it. The Pauline epistles illustrate this hope:

> Let us rejoice in hope of the glory of God (Rom. v, 2).
> ... I reckon that the sufferings of this present time are not worthy to be compared with the glory which shall be revealed to us-ward.
> (Rom. viii, 18)
> When Christ, who is our life, shall be manifested, then shall ye also with him be manifested in glory (Col. iii, 4).

So, with special intensity, does the First Epistle of Peter:

> But insomuch as ye are partakers of Christ's sufferings rejoice; that at the revelation of his glory also ye may rejoice with exceeding joy.
> (1 Peter iv, 13)
> When the chief shepherd shall be manifested, ye shall receive the crown of glory that fadeth not away (1 Peter v, 4).

And, if this hope is less prominent in some of the later New Testament writings as a result of a greater emphasis on the presence of Christ, as already realized, it never dies away. Christ's people remain

> looking for the blessed hope and appearing of the glory of our great God and Saviour Jesus Christ (Titus ii, 13).

Such is the ardent hope of the first Christians. Their imagery is drawn from the Old Testament and the apocalyptic books. It is idle to deny that the conception is quasi-physical. The 'inheritance of the saints in light' (Col. i, 12) is a region filled with the glow of a divine radiance. But, as in the Old Testament, the quasi-physical and the ethical are not far apart; and the radiance of heaven is thought of in terms of the ethical contrast between light and darkness, 'ye were once darkness, but are now light in

THE GLORY IN THE RESURRECTION AND PAROUSIA

the Lord: walk as children of light' (Eph. v, 8). Thus the imagery of glory expresses realities that reach beyond itself. At the centre of these realities is Jesus Christ Himself; and hence the apostolic writers are concerned not to elaborate their descriptions of the heavenly glory, but to emphasize that Jesus Christ Himself is its centre. It was *His* Resurrection which begat their faith, and it is *His* appearing which awaits them,

> on whom, though now ye see him not, yet believing, ye rejoice greatly with joy unspeakable and full of glory (1 Peter i, 8).

3

The glory of the Parousia is however anticipated already in the experience of the Church. The chapters which follow will describe some of these anticipations. Just as the future does not contain the whole of the truth about the Kingdom of God, so the future does not monopolise the whole of the manifestation of the glory.

(*a*) There was the growing realization in the apostolic Church that the glory, signally linked as it was to the Resurrection and the Parousia, was also manifested in the birth, life, ministry and Passion of Jesus.

(*b*) There was also the realization that, though the full and final entry of the Christians into the glory was yet to come, they were already being brought into union with the glory by means of the work of the Holy Spirit. Without anticipating the discussion of this in later chapters of this book we may quote Saint Paul:

> we all, with unveiled face reflecting (R.V. mg. beholding) as a mirror the glory of the LORD, are transformed into the same image from glory to glory, even as from the LORD the Spirit (2 Cor. iii, 18).

and the First Epistle of Peter:

> If ye are reproached for the name of Christ, blessed are ye; because the Spirit of glory and the Spirit of God resteth upon you.
> (1 Pet. iv, 14)

(*c*) There was also the recognition, prominent in the Gospel of Saint Mark, that during His earthly ministry our Lord had

GLORY AND TRANSFIGURATION

been seen on one occasion by three disciples in that state of light and radiance which would be His in the glory beyond the Passion. The second part of this book will contain a study of the Transfiguration and of the evidence that Saint Mark regards it as a disclosure, before the Passion, of the glory which was in store for Christ and for the disciples.

In these ways the notes of anticipation and of realization break into the apostolic expectation of the future glory; and finally the fourth evangelist insists that the glory, which the Church is destined to behold in open vision, has indeed been already manifested in the historical life of Jesus and perceived by those who believed.

In expressing a future event which has already been in a sense anticipated δόξα resembles certain other words familiar in the apostolic writings. The word *Parousia*, which we are wont to connect exclusively with the second coming of Christ, does not exclude the thought of an immediate presence. 'Though . . . the primary reference is eschatological, to a definite coming that had not yet been fully manifested, it is impossible not to notice how appropriate the word was to emphasize the nearness and the certainty of that "coming". So near was it that it was not so much a "coming" as already a "presence" of the Lord with His people, a *permanent* presence moreover, which not even absence from sight for a little while could really interrupt, and which, when fully re-established, would last for ever.'[1] Similarly those words which speak of the manifestation of Christ are used both of a future consummation and of the original events of the Gospel. Thus *Epiphaneia* (sudden appearance, the dawning of light upon darkness) is used both of the appearance of Christ at the end (1 Tim. vi, 14; Titus ii, 111, 3), and also of His first coming as Saviour (2 Tim. i, 10). *Apocalypsis* (the disclosure of something at present hidden) is used of the future disclosure of Christ (1 Cor. i, 7; 2 Thess. i, 7; 1 Pet. i, 7, iv, 13) and of the sons of God in glory (Rom. viii, 19), and also of the disclosure already of the divine secret in the Gospel (Rom. xvi, 25; Eph. iii, 3). Φανεροῦσθαι (*manifestation*) is used likewise both of the second coming (Col. iii, 4; 1 Pet. v, 4; 1 John iii, 2) and of the first (1 Tim. iii, 16; Heb. ix, 26; 1 Pet. i, 20; 1 John i, 2). Epiphany, Apocalypse, Manifestation—the appearing of the divine light,

[1] George Milligan: *Saint Paul's Epistle to the Thessalonians*, p. 147.

THE GLORY IN THE RESURRECTION AND PAROUSIA

the disclosure of the divine secret, the coming before men's eyes of Christ—these are things which the Christians await with the conviction that what the future will bring is but the consummation of a past event and a present possession. Nor is it otherwise with the glory. As they worship Jesus the Lord who has been exalted into it, and as they look for the day when it is made visible, they come to realize that it has been disclosed to them and is already near to them.

CHAPTER IV

THE GLORY IN THE LIFE AND PASSION

IT IS to a future glory that the sayings of our Lord point, and it is a future glory which the apostolic Church awaits. The eschatological use of δόξα is primary both in the tradition of our Lord's teaching and in the language of the apostolic faith. Yet this language contains hints that the glory has already been anticipated in the events of the Gospel and in the experience of the Church; and in some of the New Testament writers far more than hints occur. Saint Luke affirms that there were appearances of the glory in the life and ministry of Jesus; and Saint John affirms its presence throughout His life and ministry and passion. From the glory in the Resurrection and the Parousia we are led back to the glory in the earlier events.

I

It has to be asked whether those apostolic writers who held that the glory was 'realized' in the ministry and the passion of Jesus were importing into the story a novel and illegitimate interpretation of Jesus's own teaching.

It is true that the synoptic sayings of Jesus contain no explicit reference to the divine glory—apart from the future. Yet those sayings interpret His mission in terms of a fulfilment of the Old Testament which is final and complete, and imply the coming into history of the Kingdom of God, the day of the LORD, the age of the Messiah. The note of fulfilment appears in every stratum of the tradition of the sayings of Jesus which literary criticism can detect. 'The time is fulfilled, and the kingdom of God is at hand: repent ye, and believe in the Gospel.' (Mark i, 15.) Because Jesus is casting out devils by the finger of God the Kingdom of God is here (Matt. xii, 28; Luke xi, 20). Because the prophecies concerning the blind, the lame, the lepers, the deaf, the dead and the poor are being fulfilled the Baptist need

THE GLORY IN THE LIFE AND PASSION

not look for another (Matt. xi, 4-6; Luke vii, 22-23). Something greater than the temple (Matt. xii, 6), greater than Solomon or Jonah is here (Matt. xii, 41-42; Luke xi, 31-32). The disciples are seeing and hearing the things which prophets and kings desired in vain to see and to hear (Matt. xiii, 16-17; Luke x, 23-24).

It is not therefore fanciful to see in the messianic sayings of Jesus an implicit claim that the glory of Yahveh, as Isaiah and the Psalmists foreshadowed it, is present in His own mission. No reader of the Old Testament would believe that there was a coming of the Kingdom and of the messianic age which did not include the manifestation of the glory. The reader of the Gospel narratives is not seldom reminded of the words:

> The wilderness and the solitary place shall be glad; and the desert shall rejoice and blossom as the rose . . . they shall see the glory of the LORD, the excellency of our God. . . . Then the eyes of the blind shall be opened, and the ears of the deaf shall be unstopped. Then shall the lame man leap as an hart, and the tongue of the dumb shall sing (Isa. xxxv, 1-6).

And the reader of the beginning of the Gospel story in the synoptists is set thinking of the words which are partly quoted by the evangelists:

> The voice of one that crieth, Prepare ye in the wilderness the way of the LORD, make straight in the desert a highway for our God. Every valley shall be exalted, and every mountain and hill shall be made low: and the crooked shall be made straight, and the rough places plain: and the glory of the LORD shall be revealed, and all flesh shall see it together: for the mouth of the LORD hath spoken it.
> (Isa. xl, 3-5)[1]

These passages from the Old Testament do but provide a summary and a paraphrase of the claim, inherent alike in the sayings and the actions of Jesus, that the reign of God is present in His mission. No interpretation of that mission does justice to its immediate meaning if it falls short of the affirmation:

---

[1] Matthew and Mark quote the first two verses of this passage. Luke extends the quotation to include its 'universalist' conclusion, but it is curious that he omits καὶ ὀφθήσεται ἡ δόξα κυρίου.

GLORY AND TRANSFIGURATION

Surely his salvation is nigh unto them that fear him, that glory may dwell in our land (Psa. lxxxv, 9).

Nor is the Cross excluded. The Cross is not a tragic interruption of the messianic work of Christ: His sayings set the Cross within that work as an integral part of it in accordance with the Father's purpose (cf. Mark viii, 31; x, 45; xiv, 21, 24). The point has never been better stated than by Dr. William Manson: 'If Jesus throughout his work was conscious of standing in a circle of crisis, in which the powers of the world to come were seen to be breaking in all around him, he cannot when the prospect of death casts its shadow upon the scene have thought of that event in purely natural terms or in dissociation from the purpose and power of God which were working with him. Such a synthesis of ideas seems at any rate to leap from the heart of the striking saying recorded by Saint Luke which has surely the aspect of an authentic utterance of Jesus: "I came to cast fire on the earth, and how I would it were already kindled. But I have a baptism to be baptized with, and how oppressed I am till it is brought to pass" (Luke xii, 49. 50).'[1] The synthesis of the messianic work of Christ and the Passion of Christ goes back to Christ's own teaching. If 'glory' is rightly ascribed to the former, it cannot ultimately be withheld from the latter. The realization of this in the consciousness of the apostles was a slow process: but the truth was there in the beginning, implicit in the words and actions of our Lord.

2

It is *Saint Luke* who first tells of how the glory of God is made visible in the story of the birth and ministry of our Lord; and it is partly his theological insight and partly his love for the imagery of the Septuagint that leads him to do this.

At the annunciation the angel says to Mary:

The Holy Ghost shall come upon thee, and the power of the most high shall overshadow thee: wherefore also that which is to be born shall be called holy, the Son of God (Luke i, 35).

---

[1] W. Manson: *Jesus the Messiah*, pp. 125-6.

The word translated 'overshadow', ἐπισκιάζειν, is also used of the overshadowing cloud at the Transfiguration.[1] It is however at the Nativity that the word δόξα first occurs. While the shepherds were in the fields by night

> an angel of the Lord stood by them, and the glory of the Lord shone round about them (Luke ii, 9).

No doubt Saint Luke is thinking of a quasi-physical manifestation.[2] And the shepherds catch the strains of a heavenly host singing:

> Glory to God in the highest,
> And on earth peace among men in whom he is well pleased.
> (Luke ii, 14)

At the presentation of Christ in the temple Simeon hails him as:

> Thy salvation....
> A light for revelation to the Gentiles
> And the glory of thy people Israel (Luke ii, 30–32).

It is not certain whether 'light' and 'glory' are both in apposition to 'salvation', or whether 'revelation' and 'glory' go together in dependence upon 'light'. But the former seems more probable. Christ is light to the Gentiles, glory to Israel.

At the Transfiguration Saint Luke returns to this theme. He says specifically that on the mount

> they saw his glory (Luke ix, 32),

and it is he among the evangelists who deliberately makes the connection between the Transfiguration and the Cross explicit by relating that Moses and Elijah

> appeared in glory and spake of his decease which he was about to accomplish in Jerusalem (Luke ix, 31).

After the Transfiguration Saint Luke describes the journey of 'the Lord' [sic] towards Jerusalem as a kind of royal progress.

---

[1] In the LXX ἐπισκιάζειν is used once of the glory in the tabernacle (Ex. xl, 35), twice of the protection of God (Ps. xc, 4; cxxxix, 8), and once of glory casting its light (Prov. xviii, 11).
[2] Helmud Kittel classes Luke ii, 9, with Luke ix, 31, and Rev. xviii, 1, as instances of 'das visionare Lichtphänomen', *Die Herrlichkeit Gottes*, p. 190.

GLORY AND TRANSFIGURATION

Steadfastly setting his face towards the city he sends 'messengers before his face into every city whither he himself would come' (ix, 51-52). His couriers precede Him, heralding His coming. And when finally He enters Jerusalem the note of glory is once more struck by the throng of disciples, who

> began to rejoice and praise God with a loud voice for all the mighty works which they had seen; saying, Blessed is the King that cometh in the name of the Lord: peace in heaven and glory in the highest.
> (xix, 37-38)

Thus the Lord approaches the Passion; and, although Saint Luke never applies the word glory directly to it in the Johannine manner, he sets it in a frame of glory. Glory precedes and follows it: it is an inevitable part of the journey to glory, and the Lord says to the two disciples walking to Emmaus:

> Behoved it not the Christ to suffer these things, and to enter into his glory? (Luke xxiv, 26)

The phrase 'his glory', as applied to Christ, is Lucan. It occurs three times (ix, 26;[1] ix, 32; xxiv, 26), and significantly shews that the evangelist thinks of the divine glory in the mission of Christ as being 'the glory of Christ'.

Saint Luke is not far from the final Johannine interpretation of the life of Christ as a manifestation of glory from first to last. But on the other hand this interpretation is, as we have seen, not far from the implicit meaning of the sayings and deeds of Christ as the earliest traditions present them.

3

It was less easy for the apostolic writers to reach the conviction that the *Passion* of our Lord was a part of His glory. It was a hard road along which they had to travel from their sense of revolt at the Cross as scandal and folly to their belief that the Cross is the power of God. Several factors played their part. (1) There were the seeds already sown by our Lord in His own

---

[1] Where Mark viii, 38, has 'when he cometh in the glory of his Father with the holy angels', Luke ix, 26, has 'when he cometh in his own glory and the glory of the Father and of the holy angels'.

THE GLORY IN THE LIFE AND PASSION

teaching about the necessity of His death. (2) There was the influence of the fifty-third chapter of Isaiah which shewed how the sufferings of Christ lay within the saving activity of God.[1] (3) There was the experience of suffering in the Christian life. By finding that to suffer for Christ was a glorious privilege Christians could enter into some realization of the glory of Christ's own suffering. Because Saint Paul can say, from the vivid experiences of his own discipleship: 'But far be it from me to glory, save in the Cross of our Lord Jesus Christ' (Gal. vi, 14), he is able to teach that the Cross is 'the power of God and the wisdom of God' (1 Cor. i, 24).

The roots of the doctrine that the Cross is glory are vividly disclosed in the *First Epistle of Saint Peter*. Elementary and undeveloped as the theology of this book is, it shows something of the way in which the glory and the Passion came to be drawn together in the consciousness of the early Christians. If (as the present writer thinks) Saint Peter himself wrote the book with the help of Silvanus many of its features are made intelligible as the reflection of his own personal knowledge of Christ's sufferings in the flesh and of the conflicts of his own discipleship. If another wrote the book, the validity of its testimony to the experience of the apostolic Church remains.

1. Peter is addressed to Christians who are well acquainted with suffering, and are likely to experience suffering still more acute in the very near future. But they are within the living hope to which, in their baptism, they were begotten again by the Resurrection of Jesus Christ (i, 3); and this hope points forward to the glory that awaits them at the Parousia (i, 7; iv, 13; v, 4; v, 10). On this hope Saint Peter bids them fix their minds, and so possess 'a sense of perspective in which they can see and feel the contrast between the shortness of time and the lightness of their affliction here, and the infinite and overwhelming glory beyond'.[2] But, looking back, they must also remember that Christ Himself suffered; and he recalls to them, with vivid reminders of what he himself saw as an eyewitness, the sufferings of their Master as an example for them to follow. With Christ's own sufferings behind them and with a crown of glory awaiting

[1] Cf. ὑψωθήσεται, δοξασθήσεται in the LXX of Isaiah lii, 13.
[2] E. G. Selwyn: *The First Epistle of Saint Peter*, p. 79.

41

them, their own suffering is indeed transformed. It is part of the road to glory, it can be borne even with rejoicing (i, 8; iv, 13). Thus, without saying in so many words that the suffering of Christ or of the Christians *is* glory, Saint Peter writes as if the light of the Parousia-glory were thrown back upon the path of the suffering Church.

> If ye are reproached for the name of Christ blessed are ye; because the Spirit of glory and the Spirit of God resteth upon you (iv, 14).

The last clause is notoriously difficult, and its interpretation is discussed in Appendix A of this book. But whether we follow the R.V. or whether we read, following Selwyn, 'the presence of the glory, yea the spirit of God rests upon you', it is plain that in some way a foretaste of glory is given to the Christians in their present sufferings. The earnest of the Spirit is the earnest of the glory which is to be theirs. Hence always Christians may rejoice with a joy that is 'unspeakable and endowed with glory from above (χαρᾷ ἀνεκλαλήτῳ καὶ δεδοξασμένῃ)' (i, 8).

Thus Saint Peter exhorts his readers to see their sufferings in a double relation: to Christ's own sufferings in the past, and to the glory of the Parousia in the future. The writer has a twofold source of authority for his teaching: he is

> a witness of the sufferings of Christ, who am also a partaker of the glory that shall be revealed (v, 1).

It is possible that this last phrase, ὁ τῆς μελλούσης ἀποκαλύπτεσθαι δόξης κοινωνός, does not mean (as it is commonly understood) 'one who will be a partaker of the glory that shall be revealed', but (as the language strictly suggests) 'one who is or has been already a partaker of the glory that shall be revealed'—a reference to the Transfiguration where Saint Peter had a foretaste of the future glory.[1] The theme of the Epistle consists well with the testimony of an apostle who saw both the glory on the 'holy mount' and something of the events of Good Friday. Be that as it may, there is no book in the New Testament which

---

[1] E. G. Selwyn: *The First Epistle of Saint Peter*, ad. loc., following Estius and Alford. The usual explanation 'extends the future sense expressed in τῆς μελλούσης to cover κοινωνός as well, as though ἐσόμενος were to be understood with it'.

THE GLORY IN THE LIFE AND PASSION

more vividly shews us the links which connect the glory with both the Cross and the Parousia: and the links were forged in the teaching of Jesus and in the apostolic experience of suffering and hope.

In a different way the *Epistle to the Hebrews* shews the link between Cross and glory. No writer dwells more upon the heavenly life of our Lord, as with considerable borrowing from the Alexandrine type of Platonic thought he depicts the world of unseen realities wherein our Lord is high priest for ever. Equally, no writer recalls more vividly our Lord's earthly life— His temptations, His growth in obedience, His strong crying and tears, His godly fear. It is in his power to relate these two aspects of our Lord to one another that his greatness as a theologian lies, and it is no small part of his greatness that he relates *both* aspects to the glory.

The writer begins with the contemplation of the divine status of our Lord, who is

> the effulgence of his glory, and the very image of his substance (i, 3).

Such He is in eternity. And, His mission in time which issued in 'the purification of our sins' being complete,

> he sat down at the right hand of the majesty on high (i, 4).

He reigns upon the heavenly throne, with a kingship and a Sonship, such as could be ascribed to no angel and such as finds fitting expression in the Psalmist's words:

> Thou art my son, this day have I begotten thee,
> Thy throne, O God, is for ever and ever,
> Sit thou on my right hand until I make thine enemies the footstool of thy feet.

Thus the heavenly king, son, priest is hailed.

But the mission of our Lord was on earth. As man He lived and died in order to bring the human race to the destiny of glory which the eighth Psalm had described:

> Thou madest him a little lower than the angels:
> Thou crownest him with glory and honour, and didst set him over the work of thy hands,
> Thou didst put all things in subjection under his feet.

Such is mankind's destiny. But, as the writer reminds us, we do not yet see it realized: 'we see not yet all things made subject unto him'. But the first steps have been accomplished, for

> we behold him who hath been made a little lower than the angels, even Jesus, because of the suffering of death crowned with glory and honour, that by the grace of God he should taste death for every man. For it became him, for whom are all things, and through whom are all things, in bringing many sons unto glory, to make the author of their salvation perfect through sufferings. (ii, 9–10.)

Applying the imagery of Psalm viii now to Jesus Himself the writer sees the sufferings of Jesus as the necessary prelude to the bringing of mankind to its destiny of Sonship and glory. In so doing he connects the death of Christ and the glory. But how? The precise interpretation of δόξῃ και τιμῇ ἐστεφανωμένον ὅπως χάριτι θεοῦ ὑπὲρ παντὸς γεύσηται θανάτου is difficult. Do the words mean that the crowning with glory followed the Passion and made it efficacious for every man? Westcott so understood the clause: 'the glory which followed the death marked its final efficacy'. Or do the words mean that Christ went to His death as one already crowned and glorious? Bruce, Nairne and others have followed this bolder interpretation: 'while it is a humiliation to die, it is glorious to taste death for others' (Bruce).

On either interpretation of this sentence we are near, on the latter interpretation we are very near, to the Johannine doctrine of the identity of Cross and glory. The imagery is rich in its suggestiveness. It has been connected by some with the picture of garlanded victims being led to sacrifice.[1] Others have been irresistibly reminded of the Johannine story of the trial of Jesus before Pilate. 'Behold your king': 'Behold the man' says Pilate as Jesus stands robed in purple and crowned with thorns; and the Epistle to the Hebrews, with its presentation of Christ as king enthroned at the right hand of God and as Man fulfilling the destiny depicted in the eighth Psalm, provides the Christian

---

[1] E.g. W. H. G. Holmes in the *Indian Church Commentary* on Hebrews, ad. loc. In a letter to the present writer Fr. Holmes says: 'I had so often seen in India the garlanded victims being led to sacrifice, and I assumed that this picture must be in the mind of the writer of Hebrews, for he too must also have seen the same.'

THE GLORY IN THE LIFE AND PASSION

answer. The 'Ecce Homo' of Pilate has its counterpart in the 'Ecce Homo' of Christian faith: 'we behold him, even Jesus crowned with honour and glory.'

In all these ways the apostolic writers shew us the growing conviction of the Church that the Passion of Jesus belongs to the glory no less than the Resurrection and the Parousia. If 1 Peter and Hebrews afford striking illustrations of this conviction as it moves towards maturity, the last word is with Saint John. But before his doctrine of the glory is described it is necessary to examine first the distinctive teaching of Saint Paul in all its aspects.

CHAPTER V

THE GLORY IN THE TEACHING OF SAINT PAUL

I

SAINT PAUL was a Hebrew of Hebrews, and nowhere is this more plain than in his thinking about the glory of God. While there are, at most, only a very few traces in his writings of the rabbinic doctrine of the Shekinah, we find him alluding not seldom both to the scriptural doctrine of the *kabod* and to the Apocalyptic hope of the messianic glory. To him the glory of God is the character and power of God, known in creation, in providence and in history. If he does not say in so many words that 'the heavens declare the glory of God' he certainly believes it, 'for the invisible things of him since the creation of the world are clearly seen, being perceived through the things that are made, even his everlasting power and divinity' (Rom. i, 20). But mankind is unresponsive. Idolaters 'changed the glory of the incorruptible God into the likeness of the image of corruptible man' (Rom. i, 23), and the whole race 'fell short of the glory of God' (Rom. iii, 23).[1] So the devout Pharisee looks forward to the messianic glory that is to be, and he longs for the entrance of his race into the radiance of the messianic age.

But how can this be? His sense of the divine holiness and the sinfulness of man prevents any easy solution. The problem of man's glorifying is one with the problem of man's justification; and the only answer is in the grace of God who in the events of the Gospel brings both God's glory and God's justification with-

---

[1] Saint Paul is no doubt alluding here to the rabbinic idea that Adam was created with a ray of the divine glory on his face, and that this was one of the six things lost at the fall. There was a brief restoration of the ray of glory at Sinai, but it was lost again through Israel's infidelity. The rabbinic idea suggests for us is the important truth that the glorifying of man in the new creation is the realization of his true meaning in the old.

THE GLORY IN THE TEACHING OF SAINT PAUL

in reach of man. In a number of passages the connection between glory and justification is suggested:

> for all have sinned, and fall short of the glory of God; being justified freely by his grace through the redemption that is in Christ Jesus. (Rom. iii, 23-24)
>
> Being therefore justified by faith . . . let us rejoice in hope of the glory of God (Rom. v, 1-2).
>
> whom he justified, them he also glorified (Rom. viii, 30).

Nowhere is the connection more plain than in 2 Corinthians iii, where Saint Paul contrasts the two covenants:

> For if the ministration of condemnation is in glory, much rather doth the ministration of righteousness exceed in glory (2 Cor. iii, 9).

The transitory glory of the old covenant is surpassed by the abiding glory of the new covenant, since the latter is a covenant of righteousness by which the justification of men is made effective.

There is thus in the thought and language of Saint Paul a certain fusion between a quasi-physical conception of light and radiance, and a view of the glory as the power and character of God in redemption through Christ. And the former conception seems to be dominated by the latter.[1] Neither aspect of Saint Paul's thought can probably be excluded from the pregnant phrase: 'the glory of God in the face of Jesus Christ'. Here we seem to be at the heart of Saint Paul's doctrine. The phrase occurs in a description of the work of the apostles in the preaching of the Gospel:

> But and if our Gospel is veiled, it is veiled in them that are perishing: in whom the god of this world hath blinded the minds of the unbelieving, that the light of the gospel of the glory of Christ, who is the image of God, should not dawn upon them. For we preach not ourselves, but Christ Jesus as Lord, and ourselves as your servants for Jesus' sake. Seeing it is God, that said, Light shall shine out of darkness, who shined in our hearts, to give the light of the knowledge of the glory of God in the face of Jesus Christ (2 Cor. iv, 3-6).

---

[1] The relation of the two conceptions is well discussed by Helmud Kittel: *Die Herrlichkeit Gottes*, pp. 192-221. He speaks of 'die Sublimierung der Machtidee in der Rechtfertigung—δόξα'.

GLORY AND TRANSFIGURATION

In contrast with the darkened minds of the heathen, whom Satan has blinded, there is the illumination which the Gospel brings. The content of the Gospel is 'the glory of the Messiah'; and because the Messiah is the εἰκών, or perfect representation of God, 'the glory of the Messiah' and 'the glory of God' are identical. The illumination brought by the Gospel is likened to a new creative act of God. God, who said: 'Let there be light' and caused the light first to appear from the primeval darkness, has by a new creation set in the hearts of men the illumination brought by the glory of God in the face of Jesus. It is both an external event, as when Saint Paul says: 'Have I not seen Jesus our Lord?' (1 Cor. ix, 1); and an inward act of grace, as when he says: 'it pleased God to reveal his Son in me' (Gal. i, 16).

The decisive event which inaugurated Saint Paul's belief in 'the glory of the Messiah' was of course the appearance of the risen Jesus to him on the journey to Damascus. He saw 'a light from heaven above the brightness of the sun' (Acts xxvi, 13; cf. ix, 3, xxii, 6): he received a commission as an apostle to the Gentiles 'to open their eyes that they may turn from darkness to light, and from the power of Satan unto God' (Acts xxvi, 18). It has been thought that the vision at his conversion accounts for the phrase here: 'the glory of God in the face of Jesus Christ'. But this is not certain.[1] Saint Paul may have in mind not an experience peculiar to himself but the illumination which the Gospel has brought to all the apostles and to their converts.

For while the influence of the conversion experience upon Saint Paul's conception is probable and the background of the quasi-physical radiance in the Apocalyptic books is certain, the dominant idea in Saint Paul's teaching is that the *kabod* of the living God has been unfolded in the Gospel history and in its results. How inclusive the conception is, the later Epistles specially shew us. Here the sphere of the glory is the whole range of

---

[1] The connection between Saint Paul's idea of glory and his experience on the Damascus road is strongly emphasized by H. A. A. Kennedy: *Saint Paul's Conception of the Last Things*, pp. 90-92. On the other hand, Schlatter denies the influence of the conversion episode even upon 2 Cor. iv, 6. 'Er hat hier nicht von der besonderen Weise seiner Bekehrung gesprochen, da er nicht einzig von sich spricht. Deshalb spricht er vom schöpferischen Vorgang, dem er die Erkenntnis Jesu verdankt, in Worten, die auch das, was seine Mitarbeiter erlebten, mit umfasst.'—*Paulus der Bote Jesu*, p. 530.

the Gospel history, and a significant connection between 'glory' and 'power' and 'riches appears'. Thus in Colossians he speaks of

> the riches of the glory of this mystery among the Gentiles, which is Christ in you, the hope of glory (Col. i, 27),

and he describes his readers as

> strengthened with all power, according to the might of his glory.
> (Col. i, 11)

And in the first chapter of Ephesians he shews how the age-long purpose of God towards the human race is summed up in the manifestation of the glory. The Christians enjoy a redemption which is

> according to the good pleasure of his will, to the praise of the glory of his grace which he freely bestowed on us in the Beloved.
> (Eph. i, 5–6)

And when the apostle prays that his readers may learn

> what are the riches of the glory of his inheritance in the saints
> (Eph. i, 18)

he addresses his prayer to

> the God of our Lord Jesus Christ, the Father of [the] glory.
> (Eph. i, 17)

It is possible that in this last phase Saint Paul is identifying 'the glory' with Jesus Christ Himself. Or it is possible that the genitive is adjectival, and that Saint Paul means 'the Father whose characteristic is glory' or 'the glorious Father'—glorious with the glory which has shone so signally in the saving work of Christ.[1]

How great has been the reversal in the attitude of Saul of Tarsus towards Jesus Christ, and how correspondingly great has been the revolution in his doctrine of the divine glory! Here, in the life, death and Resurrection of the Messiah, the hope of the entry of mankind into the radiance of the world-to-come is brought near, and at the Parousia the hope will be more than

[1] See Appendix I, 'Jesus Christ, the Glory and the Image', for a discussion of this passage and others where the possibility of an identification of Jesus Christ with 'the glory' arises.

GLORY AND TRANSFIGURATION

answered. The anxious piety of the devout Pharisee gives place to a new conviction of the sovereignty and fatherly love of God. Because God is 'the God of our Lord Jesus Christ, the Father of glory', Saint Paul knows that he lives in a world where the decisive act of salvation has already been wrought, where suffering itself is transfigured, where 'neither death nor life, nor angels, nor principalities, nor things present, nor things to come, nor height, nor depth, nor any other creature shall be able to separate us from the love of God which is in Christ Jesus our Lord' (Rom. viii, 38–9). Even as a prisoner, with the prospect of death before him, he is sure that the sovereign power of God is working out the purpose of His will with the praise of His glory as the goal.

2

Just because Saint Paul was convinced of the revelation of the *kabod* in the Messiah's work of deliverance he was the more confident in his expectation of the participation of the Christians in the radiance of the 'eschatological' glory. This part of his teaching now calls for investigation. The Lord Jesus, risen from the dead, was already in glory (cf. Phil. iii, 21), and when He returned in glory His people would enter into the glory themselves.

Exhorting you . . . to the end that ye should walk worthily of God, who calleth you into his own kingdom and glory (1 Thess. ii, 12).

God chose you from the beginning unto salvation . . . whereunto he called you through our Gospel, to the obtaining of the glory of our Lord Jesus Christ (2 Thess ii, 13–14).

Let us rejoice in hope of the glory of God (Rom. v, 2).

For I reckon that the sufferings of this present time are not worthy to be compared with the glory that shall be revealed to usward.
(Rom. viii, 18)

When Christ who is our life shall be manifested, then shall ye also be manifested with him in glory (Col. iii, 4).

Such is the hope which Saint Paul describes by the word δοξα. The imagery is that of the elect dwelling in celestial light

THE GLORY IN THE TEACHING OF SAINT PAUL

(cf., e.g. Apoc. Bar. xv, 8; 4 Ezra vii, 42). It will be both a glory of Christ which we shall see, and a glory that will enfold us.

The present life of the Christians is therefore lived in reference to the future glory. The thought of the apostles does not begin with the present and pass on to the eschatology as a kind of further stage. It begins with the eschatology, intent upon the coming Parousia; and then it perceives that the eschatology is being anticipated in the here and now, and that the glory of the Parousia seems to throw its light backwards upon the present life of the Church. We have seen how vividly the First Epistle of Saint Peter shews us the Church looking forward to the Parousia, and discovering that the glory already rests upon it in the midst of its suffering. So too Saint Paul teaches that there is an anticipated glory wrought in the Christians by the Holy Spirit as an earnest or foretaste of the glory to come.

The classic description of the glorifying of the Christians at the present hour is in 2 Corinthians iii. Saint Paul has been contrasting the old covenant and the new: the one is akin to the transitory glory upon the face of Moses, the other is akin to the abiding glory of the Gospel.

> But if the ministration of death, written and engraven on stones, came with glory, so that the children of Israel could not look steadfastly upon the face of Moses for the glory of his face; which glory was passing away: how shall not rather the ministration of the Spirit be with glory? For if the ministration of condemnation is glory, much rather doth the ministration of righteousness exceed in glory. For verily that which hath been made glorious hath not been made glorious in this respect, by reason of the glory that surpasseth. For if that which passeth away was with glory, much more that which remaineth is in glory (2 Cor. iii, 7–11).

The contrasts here made are part and parcel of Saint Paul's Gospel. If the dispensation of the law, with the condemnation of sinners as its outcome, was glorious, how much more glorious is the dispensation of the Holy Spirit with, as its outcome, the conferring of righteousness upon mankind.

But Saint Paul goes on to make a bolder claim. Here and now Christians can see the glory of God, mirrored in Jesus Christ, and can be transformed into its likeness.

GLORY AND TRANSFIGURATION

Having therefore such a hope we use great boldness of speech, and are not as Moses, who put a veil on his face, that the children of Israel should not look steadfastly on the end of that which was passing away: but their minds were hardened: for until this very day at the reading of the old covenant the same veil remaineth unlifted; which veil is done away in Christ. But unto this day, whensoever Moses is read, a veil lieth upon their heart. But whensoever it shall turn to the Lord, the veil is taken away. Now the Lord is the Spirit: and where the Spirit of the Lord is (*or* where the Spirit is Lord) there is liberty. But we all, with unveiled face reflecting as a mirror (*or* beholding as in a mirror) the glory of the Lord, are transformed into the same image from glory to glory, even as from the Lord the Spirit (*or* the Spirit which is the Lord) (2 Cor. iii, 12-18).

We need now no veil, like Moses who put a veil on his face to prevent the Israelites from seeing the glory fade away from it. But the Jews still have a veil of ignorance resting upon them—for this veil is lifted only by the Gospel of Christ. Still the veil is there, whenever they study the law in their synagogues. But when one of them turns to Christ, as a Christian convert, then the veil goes.[1] Now 'the Lord' to whom such a one turns is the Spirit of Christ; and, when the Spirit of Christ rules, freedom indeed is there. And what of ourselves? We all, with no veil over our face, have our eyes fixed upon the mirror in which the glory of God is reflected, and as we gaze on that mirror we are already being transformed into His likeness and brought, more and more, to share in the glory. This happens 'even as from the Spirit who is Lord': 'it is only to be expected when the Holy Spirit is sovereign.'[2]

---

[1] It is possible that in verse 16 περιαιρεῖται is middle; and that the sentence should be translated, 'he [the Lord] taketh away the veil'. This rendering links verse 16 to verses 17 and 18: 'the Spirit, who is Lord, removes the veil of blindness and enables men to see the glory as in a mirror'. I owe this suggestion to the Rev. C. K. Barrett.

[2] A word may be said about three difficult points in this passage. (*a*) In verse 17, 'Now the Lord is the Spirit' does not mean that Saint Paul is identifying Christ and the Spirit. 'The Lord' should be regarded as in inverted commas: ' "The Lord" in the Exodus typology is the spirit.' (*b*) In the same verse there is much to be said for the conjectural emendation of Hort, κύριον for κυρίου, i.e. 'where the Spirit is Lord, or sovereign' in place of 'where the Spirit of the Lord is'. (*c*) Of the possible interpretations of the last words of the passage (verse 18) the one followed above is the only one which really makes sense,

THE GLORY IN THE TEACHING OF SAINT PAUL

Two phrases tell of the astounding privilege of the Christians.
1. First, τὴν δόξαν Κυρίου κατοπτριζόμενοι. Does this mean that we 'reflect' or that we 'behold' the glory of the Lord? The verb can mean to shew in a mirror, or to see oneself in a mirror, or to see something else in a mirror. A.V. translates 'beholding', and so follows the ancient Latin versions which render the Greek by 'contemplantes' or 'speculantes'. R.V. translates 'reflecting', which goes back to Chrysostom and is followed by many modern scholars. There are good reasons for preferring the A.V. translation—'beholding'.[1] The Christians have before them a mirror, Christ, in whom the glory of God is reflected. Looking at this mirror they see the glory not in a far distant future, but already.

So Saint Paul claims that to see the glory is a present possibility: such is the measure of his boldness. But in an earlier reference to a mirror, in 1 Corinthians xiii, 12, Saint Paul gave a reminder that in our present seeing there is a limitation. 'Now we see by means of a mirror in a riddle, but then face to face.' The perfect vision will be only when our transformation is complete.

---

i.e. to take κυρίου as adjectival. For parallels to this use see W. L. Knox: *Saint Paul and the Church of the Gentiles*, pp. 131-32.

[1] The strongest reason for translating κατοπτριζόμενοι here as 'beholding' is provided by the use of the word in Philo *Alleg. Leg.* iii, 33. Here Moses prays Ἐμφάνισόν μοι σαυτόν, γνωστῶς ἴδω σε· μὴ γὰρ ἐμφανισθείης μοι διὰ οὐρανοῦ ἢ γῆς ἢ ὕδατος ἢ ἀέρος ἢ τινος ἁπλῶς τῶν ἐν γενέσει, μηδὲ κατοπτρισαίμην ἐν ἄλλῳ τινι τὴν σὴν ἰδέαν ἢ ἐν σοὶ τῷ θεῷ. αἱ γὰρ ἐν γενητοῖς ἐμφάσεις διαλύονται, αἱ δὲ ἐν τῷ ἀγενήτῳ μόνιμοι καὶ βέβαιοι καὶ ἀΐδιοι διατελοῖεν. Moses asks to see the image of God mirrored not in any creature but in God Himself. This passage is thought to suggest the most natural interpretation of κατοπτριζόμενοι in 2 Cor. iii, 18, [by Kittel, *Theologisches Wörterbuch*, II, 693-4, Lietzmann ad. loc., and A. E. Brooke: *Journal of Theological Studies*, Oct. 1922. W. L. Knox, however, sees the background to Saint Paul's language in a theory of philosophers that reflections in a mirror were produced by emanations from the object reflected; so the reflection of Christ's image in the Christians is produced by the coming of His Spirit to them; see *Saint Paul and the Church of the Gentiles*, pp. 131-32. The translation 'reflecting as a mirror', though the weight of probability is against it, has inspired some admirable comments: so Theodoret: ἡ καθαρὰ καρδία τῆς θείας δόξης ... κάτοπτρον γίνεται. Luther: 'wie der Spiegel ein Bild sähet, so sähet unser Herz die Erkenntniss Christi'; Bengel: 'dominus... splendorem faciei suae in corda nostra tanquam in specula inmittens' (quoted by Kittel, op cit.).

GLORY AND TRANSFIGURATION

2. As we see the mirrored glory we are changed: τὴν αὐτὴν εἰκόνα μεταμορφούμεθα ἀπὸ δόξης εἰς δόξαν, καθάπερ ἀπὸ κυρίου Πνεύματος. The sovereignty of the Spirit makes the changing possible. And of what sort is the changing? Εἰκών means image or likeness, particularly a likeness which is derived from a prototype: into the likeness of Christ we are being changed. Μόρφη means real being in contrast with outward appearance; it is in respect of our real being that we are changed. It is a transformation of the essential man; and a comment is provided in Romans xii, 2, when Saint Paul says: 'be not outwardly fashioned (συνσχηματίζεσθε) according to this world; but be ye changed in real being (μεταμορφοῦσθε) by the renewing of your mind.' And the change is from glory into glory. There is no despair, for glory is a present possession: there is no contentment, for a far greater glory is the final goal.

The glorification of Christians is no pious mysticism. It is a matter of conflict and struggle in human flesh and blood. From first to last it is realized by faith; and the receiving of the image of Christ from glory unto glory cannot be separated from the bestowal of the righteousness of God 'from faith unto faith' (Rom. i, 17).[1] It includes the imitation of Christ in outward actions (1 Cor. xi, 1), and the 'formation' of Christ in the inward man (Gal. iv, 19). It involves the continual rejection of the standards and values of this present age, in order that the will of God may be discerned (Rom. xii, 2). This means a life such as the present age may not deem to be glorious in the least. Saint Paul tells us, a little later in 2 Corinthians, what the life in glory meant for the apostles: they were 'pressed on every side, yet not straitened; perplexed, yet not unto despair; persecuted, yet not forsaken; smitten down, yet not destroyed; always bearing about in the body the dying of Jesus that the life also of Jesus may be

---

[1] Schlatter well says: 'Paulus verlässt den Standert des Glaubens nicht. . . . In der ganzen Ausführung entsteht die δόξα durch das, was der Mensch im Auftrag Gottes tut.'—*Paulus der Bote Jesu*, pp. 519-20. Cf. von Gall: 'Nach unser Stelle besteht die δόξα des neuen Bundes vor allem in der δικαιοσύνη in der Tatsache, dass die Messiasgläubigen von Gott gerechtfertigt sind, was durch den Besitz des πνεῦμα erwiesen wird, das lebendig macht. Diesen engen Zusammenhang zwischen dem neutestamentlichen Heilsgut der δικαιοσύνη und der Messianischen δόξα zeigt aufs deutlichste Rom. 3. 23.'—*Die Herrlichkeit Gottes*, p. 97.

manifested in our mortal flesh' (2 Cor. iv, 8–10). But amid these conflicts they discovered the true relation between 'a light affliction' and 'an eternal weight of glory' (2 Cor. iv, 18).

The glory is thus hidden from the world and, in a measure, hidden from the Christians who are already beginning to participate in it. But at the Parousia it will be unveiled. The hiddenness is described in the Epistle to the Colossians:

> If then ye were raised together with Christ, seek the things that are above, where Christ is, seated at the right hand of God. Set your mind on the things that are above, not on the things that are upon the earth. For ye died and your life is hid with Christ in God. When Christ, who is our life, shall be manifested, then shall ye also with him be manifested in glory (Col. iii, 1–4).

They have made Christ's life their own: but it is a hidden life in God. Lightfoot's comment is unsurpassed: 'when you sank under the baptismal water, you disappeared for ever to the world. You rose again, it is true; but you rose only to God. The world henceforth knows nothing of your new life, and (as a consequence) your new life knows nothing of the world.' But at the Parousia 'the veil which now shrouds your higher life from others, and even partly from yourselves, will then be withdrawn. The world which persecutes, despises, ignores now will then be blinded with the dazzling light of the revelation.' Visible as the Church is (the New Testament knows nothing of the 'invisible Church'), its glory is hidden until the Lord's return.

'In the words "from glory to glory",' says Kittel, 'there is the bridge between the Now and the Eschatology.'[1] The bridge is wrought by the Holy Spirit whose present activity within the Christians is the earnest of the final glory. The Holy Spirit brings into the present life the powers of the age to come (Heb. vi, 4–5). His first fruits are in the Christians, anticipating the final redemption of their body (Rom. viii, 23). He is 'the Holy Spirit of promise, an earnest of our inheritance' (Eph. i, 13–14). He is the Spirit 'in whom ye were sealed unto the day of redemption' (Eph. iv, 30). The eschatological context of the doctrine of the Spirit is fundamental: there is no separation between our vocation to the service of God in this world and

---

[1] *Theologisches Wörterbuch*, II, p. 254.

our salvation unto glory in the age to come, for these are two facets of a single mystery. 'The eschatology is active in the present life of the Christians, and the present life of the Christians is governed by the eschatology.'[1] To overlook this is to miss the secret of apostolic Christianity.

[1] Kittel, op. cit., II, p. 396.

CHAPTER VI

SAINT JOHN: THE PROLOGUE AND MINISTRY

IT DOES not lie within the scope of this book to examine the difficult problems of the historical value of the Fourth Gospel. It is the view of the writer that the Fourth Gospel contains material of high historical worth, but also a large element that is to be regarded as interpretation rather than history. Without distorting the essential character of the mission and message of Jesus the evangelist draws out their significance for the human race.

The Fourth Evangelist records the story of the Ministry, Passion and Resurrection of Jesus with the conviction that the glory of God was manifested throughout the events. Hidden from those who did not believe, it was apparent to those within the circle of faith. The Transfiguration is omitted, for the glory belongs not to any isolated episodes but to the story as a whole; and later in this book it will be suggested that in several ways the tradition of the Transfiguration left its mark upon the thought and language of the writer. His Gospel is indeed the Gospel of the glory.

I

The prologue leads up to the great affirmation:

> The Word became flesh and dwelt among us, and we beheld his glory, glory as of the only begotten from the Father, full of grace and truth (John i, 14).

But this affirmation cannot be understood apart from the opening verses:

> In the beginning was the Word, and the Word was with God, and the Word was God. . . . All things were made by him; and without him was not anything made that hath been made. In him was life; and the life was the light of men (i, 1–4).

GLORY AND TRANSFIGURATION

The manifestation of the glory of the Son of God is the climax of the activity of the Word who was in the beginning with God, created all that exists, and gave life to the whole creation and light to the human race. The event cannot be torn from its cosmic context. The glory which the disciples saw in Galilee, Jerusalem and Calvary is the glory of Him who created the heavens and the earth and made Himself known in His created works, in providence, in history, and in the redemption of Israel. All that is learnt of the glory of God from Pentateuch, psalmists, prophets, wise men and rabbis, and from the light that lighteth every man, is both fulfilled and outshone in the glory of the Word-made-flesh.

Such being his theme Saint John's outlook is not limited to the thought of his own race. He is sensitive to the longings of the Hellenistic world, and he knows that among his readers there are Greeks who would 'see Jesus'. His vocabulary often betrays his desire to make the Gospel intelligible to those who are familiar with the words and the thought of Hellenistic religion. Yet his own thought is rooted in things Jewish, and if Greeks would 'see Jesus' they can do so only by learning that 'salvation is of the Jews'. Nowhere is the Jewish imagery more palpable than in his affirmation about the glory of the Word-made-flesh.

Dr. Burney claimed that the immediate background to John i, 14 is the Palestinian rabbinism familiar in the Targums, and that Saint John makes direct use of three of the Targumists' well-known conceptions. The 'word' is the *memra*. 'Dwelt' recalls the *shekinah*. 'Glory' is the *yekara*. The Greek words (λόγος ἐσκήνωσεν, δόξαν) are understood from the Aramaic equivalents which lie behind them.

> This is evidence that, so far from owing his doctrine to an Alexandrine source, he is soaked through and through with the Palestinian Jewish thought that is represented by the Targums. Nor would the teaching of the Prologue need time for its development. Any disciple of our Lord who has heard the Targumic rendering of the O.T. in the Synagogue, and who was capable of recognizing a superhuman power shining through the Master's personality in His mighty acts, of detecting the divine voice in His teaching, and at length of apprehending that in His presence on earth God had come to dwell among men, could hardly fail to draw the inference that

SAINT JOHN: THE PROLOGUE AND MINISTRY

here was the grand fulfilment of O.T. conceptions so familiar to him through the Aramaic paraphrase.[1]

It has indeed to be remembered that each of the three conceptions did not only exist in the Targumic form, but had a threefold history: Hebraic in the Old Testament, Greek in the Septuagint and Aramaic in the Targums. And it cannot be demonstrated that Saint John was thinking of the last alone. There was the 'word of the Lord' (*dabhar*) in the Hebrew scriptures before ever the rabbinic *memra* came in sight. There were the descriptions of Yahveh dwelling in the midst of Israel (*sakan*) before ever the Targumic paraphrases introduced the word *Shekinah*. There was the Hebrew *kabod* as well as the Targumic *yekara*. And the words δόξα and σκηνή in the Septuagint, as we have seen, blend together conceptions which are separate in Hebrew and Aramaic. Thus it would be rash to dogmatize as to the precise form of ideas behind John i, 14. But a passage later in the Gospel certainly suggests the writer's familiarity with the Targums, and it is perhaps Burney's strongest argument. In John xii, 41, after the quotation of Isaiah vi, we read:

these things said Isaias when he saw his glory,

and the phrase seems to shew the influence of the Targums of Isaiah vi, 1 and vi, 5.

I saw the *yekara* of the Lord resting on his throne.
Mine eyes have seen the *yekara* of the *Shekinah* of the king of the ages.

Saint John is as familiar with the rabbinic doctrines of Palestine as with the Biblical theology that lies behind them.

Such is the background. Now for the event itself. *The Word became flesh*. The paradox of the Incarnation is set forth in the contrasted words λόγος—σάρξ, the abiding Word of God— perishing human nature. 'All flesh is as grass... the grass withereth, the flower fadeth: but the word of God shall stand for ever.' It is in this paradox that the deepest significance of the glory will be found to lie. The Word *dwelt* among us. We are reminded both of the tabernacle in the wilderness, and of the prophetic imagery of Yahveh tabernacling in the midst of His people, and of

[1] C. F. Burney: *The Aramaic Origin of the Fourth Gospel*, p. 39.

the Shekinah which He causes to dwell among them. The Targum of Isaiah lx, 2, had said: 'In thee the Shekinah of Yahveh shall dwell, and his glory shall be revealed upon thee.' The place of His dwelling is the *flesh* of Jesus. Is there a contrast between the temple, which was the symbol of God's dwelling in Israel, and the flesh of Jesus which is to supersede it? W. L. Knox rejects this idea:

> The Shekinah is so much a commonplace of Judaism that it is fantastic to read into this passage a contrast between the flesh of Jesus and the temple at Jerusalem, in which the evangelist had no interest, except in so far as its destruction proves the end of the old dispensation.[1]

But there is evidence that Judaism connected the word σκηνή and its Aramaic equivalents with the temple (cf. Targum on Hab. ii, 20; Josephus *Ant.* iii, 202, viii, 106); and Schlatter comments:

> Jesus is hereby set in the place of the temple. He brings to mankind what no temple can give them, the presence of God. It is evident that for the disciples the temple was the most holy place in all Israel; it was not a work of the Jews, it was a gift of God, the visible token of the unity of God with His people. The destruction of the temple was the most painful renunciation which their attachment to Jesus brought to the disciples. Yet the ending of the temple was not a loss, but a priceless gift of God. The divine sonship of Jesus was greater than the temple (*Der Evangelist Johannes*, p. 23).

None the less it is arbitrary to see here an exclusive or primary reference to the temple. *All* the ways of the tabernacling of God in Israel had been transitory or incomplete: *all* are fulfilled and superseded by the Word-made-flesh and dwelling among us.

'The Word dwelt among us.' Should we rather translate ἐν ἡμῖν as 'within us'? 'Within us' is indeed congruous with the final purpose of the Incarnation, for the glory will one day dwell in the disciples. But 'among us' must be the meaning here, for the glory of the Word is *seen* by the disciples: it is the object of their gaze, and is not yet within them. The indwelling must await the glorifying of Jesus by the Cross, and the mission of the Holy Spirit.

[1] *Some Hellenistic Elements in Primitive Christianity*, p. 57.

Meanwhile *we beheld his glory*. The author writes as one of the eye-witnesses of the life of Jesus. The glory is *as of an only-begotten from the Father* (R.V. margin): it is a glory congruous with His Sonship, a glory such as a Father bestows upon an only Son. Neither in history nor in eternity has He a glory that is of Himself alone, and in revealing His own glory He reveals the Father's.

The Word-made-flesh is *full of grace and truth*. The O.T. words that lie behind are 'mercy and truth'. At Sinai God revealed Himself 'plenteous in mercy and truth' (Exod. xxxiv, 6), and in the Psalmist's picture of the divine visitation:

> Surely his salvation is nigh them that fear him; that glory may dwell in our land. Mercy and truth are met together; righteousness and peace have kissed each other (Ps. lxxxv, 9–10).

Grace and *truth* summarize the ministry of our Lord as the Fourth Gospel describes it. If Grace is apparent in the works whereby life and light are given to those who believe, and Truth is apparent in the words whereby Christ makes known what He has heard from the Father, the contrast is not absolute. Grace and truth are present in works and words alike.

To the Incarnation both prophecy and law have pointed forward, and by the Incarnation both are fulfilled. Saint John goes on to tell of how both John Baptist the prophet and Moses the giver of the law yield place to the finality of Jesus Christ.

> John beareth witness of him, and crieth, saying, This was he of whom I said, He that cometh after me is become before me: for he was before me. For of his fulness we all received, and grace for grace. For the law was given by Moses; grace and truth came by Jesus Christ. No man hath seen God at any time; the only begotten Son (God only begotten, R.V. margin), which is in the bosom of the Father, he hath declared him.

Here is the answer to the old problem of the vision of God. John says here that God in Himself is invisible, a truth repeated in v, 37, 'ye have neither heard his voice nor seen his form', and again in 1 John iv, 12, 'no man hath beheld God at any time'. But the invisible God has been declared to mankind (ἐξηγήσατο, enarravit) by One who is in the bosom of the Father, God only-begotten. And so complete is this revelation of God that the

GLORY AND TRANSFIGURATION

language of vision becomes in a sense admissible: even now men *can* see God.

> he that beholdeth me beholdeth him that sent me (xii, 45).
> he that hath seen me hath seen the Father (xiv, 9).
> Now have they both seen and hated both me and my Father.
> (xv, 24)

But this is not the fullest vision. There is a vision yet to come—when the Son has been glorified with the glory which He had with the Father before the world began (xvii, 5), and the disciples are led to the vision of this glory (xvii, 24). The open vision comes only at the Lord's return, and the last word is said in the First Epistle of Saint John:

> Beloved, now are we children of God, and it is not yet made manifest what we shall be. We know that, if he shall be manifested, we shall be like him; for we shall see him even as he is (1 John iii, 2).

The sight of God, wrote Westcott, is the transfiguration of man.[1]

2

The glory of the Incarnate Word is manifested in the works and the words of His ministry upon earth. Saint John specially connects the miracles with the glory. Whereas the first three evangelists normally refer to the miracles as 'mighty works' (δυνάμεις) Saint John, though he sometimes calls them works (ἔργα) more commonly refers to them as 'signs' (σημεῖα). From a larger number to which he makes allusion he selects six for vivid description:

> The turning of water into wine (ii, 1–11).
> The healing of the nobleman's son (iv, 46–54).
> The healing of the impotent man (v, 2–9).
> The feeding of the five thousand (vi, 4–13).
> The healing of the man born blind (ix, 1–7).
> The raising of Lazarus from death (xi, 1–44).

---

[1] The variety of words for 'seeing' in the Fourth Gospel does not seem to reflect differences of theological significance. The future ὄψομαι always refers to the vision of heavenly realities (iii, 36; xi, 40; xvi, 16. Cf. 1 John iii, 2), but the other tenses of ὁράω are used of bodily sight. θεάομαι is used indiscriminately. θεωρέω is used both of bodily vision (xx, 6, 14) and of contemplation (xii, 45; xiv, 17), but always with the idea of intelligent attention and perception.

SAINT JOHN: THE PROLOGUE AND MINISTRY

He dwells upon the marvellous character of these events. The man at the pool of Bethesda has been on a bed of sickness thirty-four years; the man in the temple has been blind from birth; Lazarus has been dead four days. The purpose of the miracles is evidential, and their designed effect is seen in the words which conclude the story of the first of them:

> This beginning of signs did Jesus in Cana of Galilee, and manifested his glory; and his disciples believed in him (ii, 11).

Not only in Galilee, but in Jerusalem also the signs had this result.

> Now when he was in Jerusalem at the passover, during the feast, many believed in his name, beholding his signs which he did (ii, 23).

And at the close of the Gospel the author explains that he selected the incidents

> that ye may believe that Jesus is the Christ, the Son of God; and that believing ye may have life in his name (xx, 31).

A contrast is at once apparent between the miracles in the Synoptic Gospels and those in Saint John. In the former the reader is conscious of a sense of restraint. There are frequent records of an injunction of silence by our Lord; there is an emphasis upon the necessity of faith as a precondition of the mighty works being done, and there is a refusal to give a sign from heaven. How great indeed seems to be the difference between this picture of reserve and the open and evidential use of the miracles in Saint John's narrative as signs of the glory of the Son of God!

But a close examination shews that the contrast is far less sharp than a first impression suggests. (*a*) On the one hand there are references in the earlier gospels to the mighty works being wrought as *messianic* actions whereby the Kingdom of God is made known (Matt. xi, 2-5=Luke vii, 18-22; Matt. xii, 28=Luke xi, 20, cf. Matt. xi, 20-2=Luke x, 12-14). It is true that faith is necessary if the messianic significance of the works is to be perceived; and, where faith is absent, no 'sign from heaven' or vulgar spectacle is offered to meet the craving for sensational proofs upon its own level. None the less the works do have an evidential character.

(b) On the other hand there are more than a few traces in the Fourth Gospel of the note of restraint that is so prominent in the earlier gospels. The belief that springs merely from signs and wonders is rebuked (John iv, 48). The belief that rests upon works for works' own sake is not the higher sort of belief (John xiv, 11). And, if the first miracle at Cana manifests the glory, there is no suggestion that it does so to others besides the disciples who stand already within the circle of faith. Nowhere in the Fourth Gospel does our Lord employ the miracles to convince those who have no faith at all. They convey truth to those who have faith, and they promote and deepen faith in those who will perceive their inner meaning. Alike in the Synoptics and in the Fourth Gospel there is 'a faith that precedes the miracle and a faith that follows it'.[1]

There is in fact a real similarity between the place of the miracles in our Lord's ministry as the Synoptics and as Saint John record it. This is not to deny that some of the miracles in Saint John present a difficult historical problem. But their *rationale* in Saint John is not far removed from that which we find in the earlier documents. If the Synoptists shew the implied relation of the miracles to the Kingdom of God, Saint John shews their explicit relation to the glory of Christ.[2]

But the glory which the signs manifest is not a glory of Christ in Himself. It is the glory which the Father gives to Him as He works with the Father's glory as His motive.

Again and again the narratives shew the dependence of Christ upon the Father. It is in the knowledge of this dependence that all His works are done.

My Father worketh even until now, and I work. (v, 17).

The Son can do nothing of himself, but what he seeth the Father doing: for whatsoever things he doeth, these the Son also doeth in like manner. For the Father loveth the Son, and sheweth him all things that himself doeth: and greater works than these will he shew him, that ye may marvel (v, 19-20).

[1] R. H. Strachan: *The Fourth Gospel*, p. 4.
[2] The signs in the Fourth Gospel are discussed with great insight in the too little known work of F. D. Maurice: *The Gospel of Saint John*, 1857. See also W. F. Howard: *Christianity according to Saint John*, pp. 157-64.

In everything He depends upon the Father. If men must come to Him because He is the bread of life, it is from the Father that the life is derived (vi, 57). If all judgment is placed in His hands it is a righteous judgment because He learns it from the Father and exercises it in submission to Him (v, 30). His teaching also is not His own, but drawn from the Father who sent Him (vii, 16). His complete self-giving to the Father is interwoven with the Father's giving of all things into His hands (iii, 34-5).

It is in this mutual self-giving of the Father and the Son, expressed in the dependence and submission of the Son throughout His earthly mission, that the deepest meaning of the glory lies. Jesus realizes His own glory only as He makes Himself as nought in the quest of the glory of His Father. The contrast is therefore plain between glory in the pagan sense and glory as Jesus reveals it. Men seek the glory of personal distinction through the praise and esteem of their fellows: Jesus reveals the glory of self-giving love which is the glory of the Father and the Son.

> If I glorify myself, my glory is nothing: it is my Father that glorifieth me (viii, 54).

> How can ye believe which receive glory one of another, and the glory which cometh from the only God ye seek not? (v, 44)

> He that speaketh from himself seeketh his own glory; but he that seeketh the glory of him that sent him, the same is true, and no unrighteousness is in him (vii, 18).

Such is the glory, wherein the Father glorifies the Son and the Son glorifies the Father, alike in eternity and in history. Here we touch the heart of the Johannine theology. The glory seen in the works of Jesus is a glory whose secret the Passion ultimately discloses. It is no accident that the ministry of the signs leads on to the event of the Passion:

> when ye have lifted up the Son of Man, then shall ye know that I am he, and that I do nothing of myself, but as the Father taught me, I speak these things (viii, 28).

> Therefore doth the Father love me, because I lay down my life, that I may take it again. No one taketh it from me, but I lay it down of myself. I have power to lay it down, and I have power to take it again. This commandment received I from my Father (x, 17-18).

3

The sign of the death and the raising up of Lazarus links the ministry of Jesus with the manifestation of glory in the Passion and Resurrection. Like the earlier works of Jesus it is 'for the glory of God, that the Son of God may be glorified thereby' (xi, 4). Like them it is wrought 'to the intent ye may believe' (xi, 15). Like them it reveals the glory only to those who already stand within the circle of faith: 'Said I not unto thee, that, if thou believedst, thou shouldst see the glory of God?' (xi, 40). In all this the story takes its place with the earlier signs in the gospel; and some of the Jews see a congruity between the giving of sight and the saving of life: 'Could not this man, which opened the eyes of him that was blind, have caused that this man also should not die?' (xi, 37). But the story also points forward. Its context is the danger to the life of Jesus which is impending (xi, 8), and its sequel is the plot of the Sanhedrin to destroy Him. Hence it is virtually a parable of the glory presently to be disclosed in the death and the raising-up of Jesus Himself.

The purpose of the miracle is not to shew favours to selected friends, but to glorify God by revealing the purpose of Christ as the Resurrection and the life. The issue comes to a head in the conversation between Jesus and Martha. She affirms her belief that Lazarus will rise again at the last day, clinging to this remote prospect as the sole ground of comfort. Jesus immediately confronts her with the truth that He is the Resurrection and the life: to accept Him in the allegiance of faith is to pass at once from death into life. Does Martha believe this? She confesses at once her belief in 'the Christ, the Son of God, even he that cometh into the world' (xi, 27). She sees the destinies of her brother and herself caught up, as it were, into the mission of the Messiah. The faith which He elicits from her is not a conviction that He will render a favour, but a faith in Him as the Life. Because she so believes she will be able to perceive in the miracle neither a favour nor a wonder—but *the glory of God*.

The final drama of the glory is now begun. Jesus rides into Jerusalem upon the colt—an event which the disciples will understand only 'when Jesus was glorified' (xii, 16). But, before the act of the glorifying is completed, Jesus unfolds something of its

SAINT JOHN: THE PROLOGUE AND MINISTRY

meaning first to the people in Jerusalem and then to the apostles in the Upper Room.

To the people in Jerusalem the glory is described in close connection with the judgment. The occasion is the approach of certain Greeks who desire to see Jesus. Their approach draws from Jesus words about the necessity of the Cross, for the gathering in of 'other sheep which are not of this fold' (x, 16) can only be through the willingness of the shepherd to lay down his life on their behalf (x, 17). Hearing therefore that the Greeks are seeking Him Jesus says:

> The hour is come that the Son of Man should be glorified. Verily, verily, I say unto you, Except a grain of wheat fall into the earth and die, it abideth by itself alone; but if it die, it beareth much fruit. He that loveth his life loseth it; and he that hateth his life in this world shall keep it unto life eternal. If any man serve me, let him follow me; and where I am there shall also my servant be: if any man serve me, him will the Father honour (xii, 23-26).

Jesus is making the first explicit identification of the Passion and the glory. So hard is the paradox that Jesus gives three illustrations to help his hearers to understand. (i) The seed must die that it may be fruitful. (ii) The disciple who clings to his life shall lose it, but if he loses it he will find it in eternity. (iii) The man who would serve Jesus must follow Him, and be wherever Jesus is and so receive the honour which the Father gives. The last illustration throws light upon the words in the prayer of consecration: 'I will that, where I am, there they may be with me also, that they may behold my glory which thou gavest me.' (xvii, 24). The paradox that Passion and glory are one will be learnt only in the practical obedience of discipleship.

Meanwhile the human soul of Jesus shrinks from what lies before Him.

> Now is my soul troubled; and what shall I say? Father save me from this hour. But for this cause came I unto this hour. Father glorify thy name. There came therefore a voice out of heaven saying, I have both glorified it and will glorify it again. The multitude therefore, that stood by, and heard it, said that it had thundered: others said, An angel hath spoken to him. Jesus answered and said: This voice hath not come for my sake, but for your sakes (xii, 27-30).

GLORY AND TRANSFIGURATION

Here is the Johannine counterpart to the story of Gethsemane. Let the terrible hour be averted—nay, let the Father's name be glorified. (Bengel's comment is unsurpassed: 'concurrebant horror mortis et ardor oboedentiae.') But here also is the counterpart to Mount Hermon, for a voice from heaven is heard telling the bystanders that in the obedience of the Son the Father has glorified and will glorify His name.

But with the glory there is the judgment:

> Now is the judgment of the world: now shall the prince of this world be cast out. And I, if I be lifted up from the earth, will draw all men unto me (xii, 31–32).

The Passion, whose glory is learnt only by those who believe, is the judgment upon the world which does not believe. 'Lifted up' recalls both the brazen serpent in the wilderness (cf. iii, 14) and the servant of Yahveh who will be lifted up and high exalted (Isa. lii, 12). The serpent, hideous to look upon, was the means of healing: the servant, with no beauty that men should desire him, brings deliverance from sin. To the world, judgment: to those who believe, glory: this is the paradox of Calvary.

With the thought of the tragedy of unbelief and the certainty of judgment Saint John brings to a close his record of the public teaching of Jesus. Isaiah had foretold the unbelief of the Jews, when he spoke of the blinding of their eyes and the hardening of their hearts at the time when, in his vision in the temple, he saw the glory of Christ. And now among the Jews there are some who believe, even from the Pharisees; but they dare not confess it, for they

> loved the glory of men more than the glory of God.

Thus has the Incarnate Word divided men, and sifted those who are so bent upon the glory that they receive one from another that they seek not the glory that comes from the only God (cf. v, 44).

CHAPTER VII

SAINT JOHN: THE SUPPER AND PASSION

IN CONTRAST to the unbelieving world which stands under the judgment of God there is, at the supper, the apostolic company to whom the glory of God is manifested. The feet-washing, the discourses and the prayer of consecration unfold the meaning of the glory and the path along which the apostles must journey if they would come to share in it.

The Feet-Washing

In the story of the feet-washing the word glory does not occur, but the episode seems to give a commentary upon the glory as the Fourth Evangelist understands it.

> Now before the feast of the passover, Jesus knowing that his hour was come that he should depart out of this world unto the Father, having loved his own which were in the world, he loved them unto the end. And during supper, the devil having already put into the heart of Judas Iscariot, Simon's son, to betray him, Jesus, knowing that the Father had put all things into his hands, and that he came forth from God, and goeth unto God, riseth from supper, and layeth aside his garments; and he took a towel, and girded himself. Then he poureth water into the basin, and began to wash the disciples' feet, and to wipe them with the towel wherewith he was girded.
> (xiii, 1-5)

Jesus is performing the act of a slave (1 Sam. xxv, 41), and He does this in the consciousness that the Father has entrusted all things to Him and that He is returning to the Father from whom He came. By His servile act He is glorifying the Father, and the feet-washing so far from being a veiling or an abandoning of the glory is a manifestation to the disciples of the nature of the glory of the eternal God. In utter contrast to the glory which men 'receive one of another' (v, 44) the glory 'that cometh from the only God' (ibid.) is mirrored in the figure of Jesus girded with a towel and pouring water into the basin.

The episode has received somewhat diverse interpretations from commentators. Loisy held it to be a piece of sacramental symbolism, depicting the cleansing of the members of the Church in the Eucharist. Lagrange on the other hand urged that the meaning is simple, and that we should see in the event no sacramental symbolism but an example in humility. But the antithesis between an act of humility and an act of cleansing seems to be a false one. Humility is indeed the lesson, and the whole lesson of the event. But it is the humility of the Son of God who knew that 'his hour was come' (xiii, 1), and the act foreshadows the humility of the Passion: only after the Passion will Peter understand what is now happening (xiii, 7). And the Passion as the supreme act of humility will be no less the supreme means of the cleansing of mankind. The feet-washing prefigures it, both in its humility and in its cleansing. It is both truth and grace.

The feet-washing ended, Jesus speaks to the apostles of the sovereignty which it reveals, and of the mission of the Church in relation to that sovereignty.

> Ye call me, Master and Lord: and ye say well; for so I am. If I then, the Lord and the Master, have washed your feet, ye also ought to wash one another's feet (xiii, 13–14).

From the sovereignty of the Christ there flows the sovereignty of the Church which represents Him:

> Verily, verily, I say unto you, He that receiveth whomsoever I send receiveth me; and he that receiveth me receiveth him that sent me (xiii, 20).

But the sovereignty is grounded in the Lord's humility:

> Verily, verily, I say unto you, A servant is not greater than his lord; neither he that is sent greater than he that sent him (xiii, 16).

Is there not here a commentary upon the words which come in the Prayer of Consecration: 'the glory which thou hast given me, I have given unto them' (xvii, 22)?

SAINT JOHN: THE SUPPER AND PASSION

The Betrayal and the Glory

The perfection of the feet-washing scene was marred by the presence of a traitor: 'ye are clean, but not all', 'I speak not of you all'. Now, troubled in spirit, Jesus announces to the twelve that there is a traitor among them; and, after the tense moments which follow, Judas departs into the night. 'The unclean went out,' wrote Augustine, 'and the rest remained with the cleanser.'

The episode begins and ends with references to our Lord which are in sharp contrast. Before the announcement of the traitor,

> when Jesus had thus said, he was troubled in spirit,

and after the departure of the traitor

> when therefore he was gone out, Jesus saith, Now is the Son of Man glorified.

Troubled in spirit—glorified: ἐταράχθη–ἐδοξάσθη: the same contrast had appeared when Jesus prayed: 'Now is my soul troubled—ἐταράχθη. . . . Father glorify thy name—δόξασόν. The thought of the traitor's presence casts the soul of Jesus into anguish, the departure of the traitor finds Jesus conscious of the glory which has begun.

> When therefore he was gone out, Jesus saith, Now is the Son of Man glorified, and God is glorified in him; and God shall glorify him in himself, and straightway shall he glorify him (xiii, 31-32).

The first clause speaks of a past event. It is well known that in Hebrew idiom the aorist can be used in anticipation of a future action (cf. Gen. xv, 18: 'I have given thee'; lxx: 'I will give thee'). But here is more than an idiom of anticipation. 'At the moment when Judas went out, charged to execute his purpose, the Passion as the supreme act of self-sacrifice was virtually accomplished.' (Westcott) Already there had been 'the decisive act by which the Passion had been embraced'. Already God is glorifying the Son of Man and is Himself being glorified by the Son of Man's obedience. But the latter pair of clauses look beyond the Passion, for the words 'God shall glorify him in himself' refer to the subsequent entrance of the Son of Man into the transcendent glory of God in His risen and exalted state. It is right for us in this way to distinguish between the glory in the Passion in the first two clauses, and the glory beyond the Passion in the latter: the distinction recurs in xvii, 1 and 5. But there is an inseparable unity between the two stages, which are indeed two stages only in man's apprehension of a single mystery. 'Even as God was glorified in the Son of Man, as man, when He took to himself willingly the death which the traitor was preparing, so also it followed that God would glorify the Son of Man in his own divine being, by taking up his glorified humanity into fellowship with Himself.' (Westcott)

But at the moment the disciples are conscious only of the bitter separation in the departure of Jesus to His death. In this death He is utterly isolated. He has told the Jews, and now He tells the disciples 'whither I go, ye cannot come'. But, though He will leave them in the midst of the world from which He is going, He bequeathes to them a bond. This bond is the new commandment that they will love one another even as He has loved them. And the chapters which follow show that the command to love one another as Christ has loved them is inseparable from the entrance into them of Christ's own love, the love of the Father and the Son in the Passion (xvii, 26).

Peter cannot follow now. There can be no imitation of Jesus until first there has been the receiving of the judgment and the love which the Passion brings. Peter shall follow afterwards.

The Going to the Father

There follows the last Discourse, whose theme is the new divine order which will ensue from the departure of Jesus to the Father.

The scene is tense with the perplexity of the disciples at the thought of the imminent departure of their master. Their perplexity has its root not only in a natural and selfish fear of what lies ahead nor in a passionate loyalty to Jesus, but in a feeling that His departure contradicts the message which they have been slowly learning from Him. For they have learnt to depend upon *Him*, to find *His* words and works to be the source of eternal life, to know *Him* to be the light wherein they can walk so long as *He* is with them. They have made their own a discipleship which might well find utterance in the words: 'Lord, it is good for us to be here'; and now they are 'afraid as they enter into the cloud'.

Yet the departure of Jesus is necessary for them, since, by clinging to His visible presence, they are in peril of missing two truths which He desires to bring home to them.

1. Hitherto He has been with them where they are, sharing in the circumscribed conditions and relationships of their earthly life. But it is His mission to lead them to be with Him where He is, sharing in a unity with Him uncircumscribed by touch and sight. 'As yet it was hardly possible for them to feel the difference between His being with them where they were, and their being with Him where He was . . . *that* was the transition now coming, the transition from a presence taking its character from their circumstances to a presence taking its character from His.'[1] In the new era which will follow His departure He will receive the disciples, 'that where I am, there they may be also' (xiv, 3); and while the disciples will find mansions ($\mu o \nu a \iota$) in the Father's house, the Father and the Son will come and make their dwelling ($\mu o \nu \acute{\eta}$) in the disciples (xiv, 23).

2. The glory of Christ, to which the disciples have been clinging, is not His own: He seeks the Father's glory and has always sought it. And He would lead them beyond their belief in Him, or rather in and through their belief in Him, to a true belief in the Father. The more therefore they cling to His visible presence the harder it is for them to learn that the end of discipleship is 'not a cult of Jesus but a faith in God' (Hoskyns).

These things are unfolded in the discourse, and thrice in chapters xiv–xvi the word 'glorify' occurs.

1. The first occasion is when Jesus is speaking of the greater works and the more efficacious prayer of the disciples as a result of His departure. The end of this will be the *Father's* glory.

> Verily, verily, I say unto you, he that believeth on me, the works that I do shall he do also; and greater works than these shall he do; because I go unto the Father. And whatsoever ye shall ask in my name, that will I do, that the Father may be glorified in the Son.
> (xiv, 12–13)

---

[1] F. J. A. Hort: *The Way: the Truth: the Life*, p. 14. Hort's exposition of this theme is one of the great passages in English theological writing.

GLORY AND TRANSFIGURATION

2. The second occasion is at the close of the allegory of the vine and the branches. Here too the goal of the disciples' union with Christ is the *Father's* glory.

> I am the vine, ye are the branches; he that abideth in me, and I in him, the same beareth much fruit: for apart from me ye can do nothing.... Herein is my Father glorified that ye bear much fruit; so shall ye be my disciples (xv, 5, 8).

3. On the third occasion where the word 'glorify' is used Jesus unlocks the secret. It is the Paraclete who will enable all these things to be.

> He shall glorify me: for he shall take of mine, and shall declare it unto you. All things whatsoever the Father hath are mine: therefore said I, that he taketh of mine, and shall declare it unto you.
> (xvi, 14–15)

The entire content of the good things which Jesus is predicting may be summed up as the glorifying of Christ by the Holy Spirit. The glorifying includes all that the Holy Spirit will do. He will teach the apostles, and bring the words of Jesus to their remembrance (xiv, 26). He will bear witness to Jesus in the midst of a persecuting world, and enable the apostles to bear witness (xv, 26–27). He will dwell in the apostles, and be the means of Christ's own coming to them (xiv, 17–18). He will convict the world concerning sin and righteousness and judgment (xvi, 8–11). He will guide the apostles into all the truth (xvi, 13). He will declare to them 'the things that are coming'— the events that will follow Christ's departure (xvi, 13). In all this He will glorify Christ. He cannot add to Christ's unsearchable riches: He will make them known and understood and all-powerful in human history, as the splendour of Christ is more and more reflected in the lives of men.

As the work of the Son in glorifying the Father has sprung from His utter submission to the Father and from His constant receiving from the Father all that the Father wills to give to Him, so also the work of the Spirit in glorifying the Son will spring from the Spirit's utter dependence upon the Father and the Son. As Jesus says of Himself

> all things that I heard from my Father, I have made known unto you (xv, 15),

SAINT JOHN: THE SUPPER AND PASSION

so He says of the Spirit

what things soever he shall bear, these shall he speak (xvi, 13).

The Son utters no message of His own but what He receives from the Father. The Spirit utters no message of His own, but what He too receives. And while the things which the Spirit receives are from the Son,

he shall take of mine,

they are from the Son only because they are also from the Father, for

all things whatsoever the Father hath are mine.

A Trinitarian doctrine of the Godhead is here inescapable. It is inescapable as touching the activity of God in history, for the glorifying of the Father by Jesus is perfected only in the glorifying of Jesus by the Spirit. It is inescapable as touching the being of God in Himself, for the sharing of the Son in all that the Father has is paralleled by the sharing of the Spirit in all that the Son has. The revelation of the glory of God to the disciples involves their coming to perceive that the Spirit is all that the Son is—namely God indeed.

The Prayer of Consecration

As the great discourse proceeds a tension is increasingly felt between the turbulence of the world, wherein Jesus is about to face death and the disciples persecution, and the peace which Jesus possesses in Himself and bids the apostles to share. This contrast stands out still more plainly in the Prayer of Jesus in the seventeenth chapter. Jesus speaks to the Father as the Father's eternal Son, and yet He speaks from the midst of a historical crisis of human flesh and blood. The prayer thus belongs both to the timeless converse of the Father and the Son, and to the conflict in time wherein the Son embraces the Father's will that He must die for mankind.[1] Yet the reader is conscious of no

[1] Cf. Loisy: 'Le fait est que la perspective du discours est assez flottante; tout s'explique sans distinction subtile, si l'on admet que Jean fait parler dans Jésus le Christ glorieux et eucharistique: par rapport au caché apparent, la mort de

GLORY AND TRANSFIGURATION

unreality or discontinuity in the words and the thought, for it is in the drama of time and history that the eternal glory is made known. If the tension between these two perspectives—the eternal and the temporal—makes the exegesis of particular sentences difficult, it does not mar the unity of the prayer as a whole.

The prayer has sometimes been called the High Priestly prayer, though this title does not seem to be earlier than the sixteenth century. If this title be used it must be remembered that nowhere in the prayer is there explicit reference to the burden of human sin or to the atmosphere of expiation connected with the day of atonement. Its tone is not the tone of the *kyrie eleison*: it is a prayer for victory uttered in the consciousness that the victory is won. A better name for it, drawn from one of its own phrases, is the prayer of consecration (Westcott, Hoskyns). Jesus consecrates Himself on behalf of His disciples. It is unto death that He consecrates Himself, and it is implicit in Saint John's teaching about sacrifice that the death is for the expiation of sin. The Prayer however dwells not upon the process of expiation, but upon the victory over the world which results from it. The true doctrine of atonement is the doctrine of *Christus Victor*: but it includes (what some of its exponents forget) expiation as the price and the means of victory.

Jesus prays concerning Himself (xvii, 1-8),[1] concerning the apostles (xvii, 9-19) and concerning those who will become believers through their teaching (xvii, 20-26).

1. *Jesus prays concerning Himself*

> Father the hour is come, glorify thy Son, that the Son may glorify thee:[2]

Jésus est à venir; dans la conception profonde et symbolique du discours, elle appartient au passé.'—*La Quatrième Evangile*, p. 802.

[1] Some commentators, e.g. Westcott, make the division not at verse 8 but at verse 4. But it appears to me that verses 6-8, though they are about the apostles and are therefore congruous with the second section of the prayer, are best taken as an expansive comment upon 'I glorified thee on the earth' in verse 4, just as verses 2 and 3 are an expansive comment upon 'that the Son may glorify thee' in verse 1.

[2] W. L. Knox cites a parallel in Greek magic, a papyrus where the adept prays to Isis, 'glorify me, as I have glorified the name of thy son, Horus'. He argues that Greek magic had borrowed this use of δόξα from Jewish sources.— *Some Hellenistic Elements in Primitive Christianity*, p. 85.

even as thou gavest him authority over all flesh, that whatsoever thou hast given him, to them he should give eternal life. And this is life eternal, that they should know thee the only true God, and him whom thou didst send, even Jesus Christ.

I glorified thee on earth, having accomplished the work that thou gavest me to do. And now, O Father, glorify thou me with thine own self with the glory which I had with thee before the world was.

I manifested thy name unto the man whom thou gavest me out of the world: thine they were, and thou gavest them to me; and they have kept thy word. Now they know that all things whatsoever thou hast given me are from thee: for the words which thou gavest me I have given unto them, and they received them, and knew of a truth that I came forth from thee, and they believed that thou didst send me.

The text is here printed so as to shew how the references to the glorifying of the Father, both in verse 1 and in verse 5, are followed by a description of the work of the mission of the Son whereby the Father is glorified. *First*, Jesus prays that in the Passion which is now imminent the Father may give glory to the Son and enable the Son to give glory to the Father. This He will do by bringing to the disciples eternal life in the knowledge of God. The godward act of glorifying the Father includes the manward act of revealing Him to men. As yet the revelation is only to a little company, but this little fragment of the human race represents a vaster potentiality, for 'all flesh' lies within the sphere of the authority which the Father gave to Him. *Second*, Jesus, who has glorified the Father throughout His entire mission on earth, asks to be given a glory beyond the glory in the Passion, a glory that is no less than the eternal glory of the Godhead. Nowhere does Saint John tell us that this glory was veiled or laid aside during the Son's incarnate life, but the Son took upon Him a truly human life in order to win by the road of a human life and death a glory that was always His own. And now He asks that the human nature (in which He prays) may be exalted into union with the Godhead. Once more, the godward act of glorifying includes the manward mission; and Jesus has glorified the Father by making the Father's name known to the apostles and by leading them to learn that His mission was from the Father.

GLORY AND TRANSFIGURATION

2. *Jesus prays concerning the disciples*

I pray for them: I pray not for the world, but for those whom thou hast given me; for they are thine: and all things that are mine are thine, and thine are mine: and I am glorified in them. And I am no more in the world, and these are in the world, and I come to thee. Holy Father, keep them in thy name which thou hast given me, that they may be one, even as we are. . . . I have given them thy word; and the world hated them, because they are not of the world, even as I am not of the world. I pray not that thou shouldest take them from the world, but that thou shouldest keep them from the evil one. They are not of the world, even as I am not of the world. Sanctify them in the truth: thy word is truth. As thou didst send me into the world, even so sent I them into the world. And for their sakes I sanctify myself, that they also may be sanctified in truth.

Not directly can Jesus pray for the world, despite the authority over 'all flesh' that has been given to Him—for the world means the pattern of human life in rebellion against God. He prays for the disciples. They belong to Him utterly—but He is on His journey to the Father, and they are left in the midst of the world. He prays that the Father may guard them securely in the name[1] which He has given to them; and that, however greatly the world may hate them because they are not of the world, they may without withdrawal from the world be kept from the evil one.

The petitions for the disciples are summarized in the words 'sanctify them in the truth'. The connection between sanctification and truth is of the utmost consequence. The disciples in their mission in the world are required to be 'not of the world' in two ways. They are to be consecrated to God in opposition to the world's self-pleasing: they are to represent the truth of God in opposition to the world's errors. The two requirements are inseparable, even as grace and truth are inseparable in the mission of Christ. Lack of consecration may corrupt their intellectual witness to the truth: woolliness of mind concerning the theology entrusted to them may betray them into a facile

---

[1] On the *Name*, see Bernard, ad. loc. The word means the revelation of God's nature with special reference to the succour which He gives to those who need it, cf. Ps. xliv, 5: 'Through thy name will we tread them under that rise up against us.'

assimilation to the world's own presuppositions. Therefore Jesus prays 'sanctify them in the truth'. There is no holiness apart from the theology which He reveals, and there is no imparting of the theology except by consecrated lives.

To this end Jesus sanctifies Himself: ὑπὲρ αὐτῶν ἐγὸ ἁγιάζω ἐμαυτον. The verb, which originates in Biblical Greek, means to set apart or dedicate and, more particularly, to dedicate as a sacrifice. The sentence 'does not mean that Jesus achieved righteousness or exercised a strict moral self-control in order that His disciples might be granted a similar righteousness; still less does it mean that Jesus made Himself righteous in order that the disciples might possess an example for their active imitation. It means that the Son of God consecrates His blameless life as an effective sacrifice on behalf of the disciples in order that they might be set forth in the world as the concrete righteousness of God . . . dedicated to the service of God even to death for his glory. The consecration of the disciples therefore depends upon the consecration of the Son of God. But the similarity rests upon a great dissimilarity: they are consecrated, He consecrated Himself and His consecration must precede theirs.' (Hoskyns, ad. loc.)

3. *Jesus prays concerning those who will believe through the teaching of the apostles*

> Neither for these only do I pray, but for them that believe on me through their word; that they may be one; even as thou, Father, art in me, and I in thee, that they also may be in us; that the world may know that thou didst send me. And the glory which thou hast given me I have given unto them; that they may be one even as we are one; I in them, and thou in me, that they may be perfected into one; that the world may know that thou didst send me, and lovedst them as thou lovedst me.

Beyond the portion of humanity which the Father has given to the Son already there is the wider company of those who will come to believe through the mission of the apostles. He prays for them; that they may be led to participate in the unity whereby the Father and the Son are one, and that by thus participating they may bring the world to the conviction that the Father sent the Son. After making this petition (verse 21) Jesus virtually repeats it with the addition of the two words 'glory' and 'love'.

GLORY AND TRANSFIGURATION

For the participation in the unity of the Father and the Son which He gives to the disciples is nothing less than their participation in the glory which the Father gives to Him. And the conviction of men that the Father sent the Son is nothing less than their recognition of the love of the Father for them, a love as great as His love for the Son.

The prayer now mounts to a plane of triumph. Jesus, abandoning the language of supplication, uses the language of sovereign purpose, saying not 'I pray' but 'I will'.

> Father, that which thou hast given me, I will that, where I am, they also may be with me; that they may behold my glory, which thou hast given me; for thou lovedst me before the foundation of the world.

Jesus wills that where He is, the disciples may be (cf. xii, 26; xiv, 3). He determines that they will dwell in the mansions of the Father's house, whither He Himself is going (cf. xiv, 2). And there is in store for them the vision of glory, not only the vision of the glory of Christ which they have seen in His earthly ministry, but the vision of the eternal glory of the Son in union with the Father. They will 'see Him as He is' (1 John iii, 2), because—in answer to the self-consecration of Jesus for them—they will have been made like Him.

Thus the prayer reaches forward into the final vision of glory. But it is uttered by the Son of Man in the midst of a stubborn and unbelieving world.

> O righteous Father, the world knew thee not, but I knew thee: and these knew that thou didst send me; and I made known unto them thy name, and will make it known; that the love wherewith thou lovest me may be in them, and I in them.

Amid the stubborn and unbelieving world there is the Church of God. Its members know whence Jesus came; and He has declared to them the protection of the Father's name and will declare it to them again, that they may be overshadowed by the love wherewith the Father loves Him.

SAINT JOHN: THE SUPPER AND PASSION

The Passion and its Sequel

The prayer is ended. The Passion begins. Throughout the narrative John shews that the prayer is being answered and the Son is being glorified. In the garden the soldiers who come to arrest Jesus fall to the ground awestruck at His majesty. In the judgment hall it is Jesus who is the judge and Pilate is his craven prisoner. Before the people Jesus is shewn forth as King, in the purple and the crown of thorns; and King indeed He is. Master of His destiny Jesus carries His own Cross to Calvary, for He has power to lay down His life and power to take it again. On Calvary He reigns, ordering the future for the mother and the disciple, crying 'it is accomplished', fulfilling the Scriptures, and freely surrendering His spirit to the Father. So the hour came that the Son of Man should be glorified, and the corn of wheat fell to the earth and died.

Calvary is no disaster which needs the Resurrection to reverse it, but a victory so signal that the Resurrection follows quickly to seal it. John thinks of the glorifying of Jesus as completed on Easter day. The glorifying accomplished, the Spirit can be given (cf. vii, 39). Coming to the apostles on the evening of 'that day' Jesus breathes on them and says: 'Receive ye the Holy Ghost.' By the breath of a new creation the Church is brought to birth and sent upon its mission: 'as the Father hath sent me, even so send I you.'

By the mission of the Church the judgment and the glory are made known to mankind, and the world can take its choice.

CHAPTER VIII

THE GLORY AND THE CHRISTIAN FAITH

IN THE previous chapters of this book the Biblical conception of the glory of God has been traced in every part of the Old Testament and the New. We have seen how the *kabod* of Yahveh includes ideas of power, character, radiance and physical accessibility which can be neither wholly disentangled nor set in historical sequence. We have seen how the Greek word δόξα finds a new meaning to express the Biblical conception in its variety and unity, and to provide a pattern upon which the New Testament writers could work. Then came the revelation of glory in the Gospel. Still the ideas of power, character, radiance and physical accessibility are included, for if the physical suggestions of glory are now made utterly subordinate to its ethical and transcendental aspects they never wholly disappear. To the last man's quest remains what it was in the days of Moses—the *seeing* of God. The Christian does not despise as carnal the ancient longing: 'Shew me, I pray thee, thy glory.'

In tracing the doctrine of the glory we have, almost unwittingly, been disclosing the pattern of the faith of the Bible. The God of the Bible is manifested in His created works, and yet He transcends them all. He rules in history with the sovereignty of His righteous purpose: He shewed His glory in delivering Israel to be His people, and though His glory cannot be circumscribed in time or place He set it in the midst of Israel as a tabernacling presence. Again and again He judged Israel for ascribing glory not to Him but to herself; and in the fullness of the times, He manifested His glory decisively in the birth, life, death and Resurrection of His Son. Once more He redeemed a people and set the glory of His presence in their midst, a glory which faith alone can discern. Again and again He has judged the new Israel for ascribing glory not to Him but to herself. And our present discerning of the glory of God by faith is not worthy to be compared to the vision of glory when we shall see Him as He is. In this glory not only redeemed humanity but all creation will share, though it now groans in bondage and awaits its deliverance into the liberty of the glory of God's children. In His glory righteousness and power are inseparably one; together with a radiance—bright so that men may receive knowledge of the truth, yet so bright that the truth is beyond their understanding.

The conception of glory illuminates every part of the structure of the Christian faith.

God

The glory of God has been disclosed in His created works. 'The heavens declare the glory of God; and the firmament sheweth his handywork' (Ps. xix, 1). In the things that are made the everlasting power and divinity of God are discernible by man, who is without excuse if he fails to give glory to Him (Rom. i, 20). But although God is known in His creation He transcends it utterly. Without Him, it cannot be: without it, His being is perfect. It is not that the existence of creatures is necessary to His glory, but that His creating them is the utterance or overflowing of a glory which eternally lacks nothing. The Biblical doctrine condemns the recurring sin whereby we worship some creature in place of the Creator, and it denies two recurring errors: the error of neglecting the *testimonia gloriae* in nature, in man and in history, and the error of treating God and the created world as co-partners mutually necessary.[1] To glorify God is both to rejoice in His works, and to own their absolute dependence upon the Creator.

It is perhaps surprising that the word *glory* does not occur in the Synoptic record of the teaching of Jesus about God. But in all that He taught about the providence, graciousness, Fatherhood and judgment of God, Jesus was implicitly speaking of the divine glory. Above all, He brought into particular prominence the Fatherhood of God: 'Father' became not one title amongst many, but *the* title by which God is named. In the Lord's Prayer

[1] This error is effectively criticized, in relation to some modern tendencies, by L. Hodgson in *The Doctrine of the Trinity*, pp. 122-34, and E. L. Mascall in *He Who Is*, pp. 105-112.

the 'name', the 'kingdom' and the 'will' of the Father comprise the Father's glory. But Jesus reveals the Father not by expounding a doctrine of universal Fatherhood, but by executing His own mission as the Son, by teaching men that God is H̩is Father and by leading them to learn of *His* sonship. Only when the mission of the Son has reached its climax in the Passion and when the Spirit of the Son has been sent into the hearts of the disciples crying 'Abba, Father', can they come to know the Father's glory.

It is thus in the revelation of the Son and in the gift of the Spirit that the Father's glory is fully disclosed. And it is disclosed in an inseparable union with the glory of the one God, Father, Son, Spirit. The obedience of Jesus to the Father in His life and death and the vindication of Jesus by the Father in the Resurrection are the disclosure within time of a glory of self-giving love which belongs to God from all eternity. 'The doctrine of the Trinity is the projection into eternity of this essential relationship, the assertion that eternally the divine life is a life of mutual self-giving to one another of Father and Son through the Spirit who is the *vinculum* or bond of love between them.'[1] 'He lives in a human way the replica of a previous mystery, without which the historic mystery would not exist. The marvels of Galilee and Judaea are possible only because God has an eternal Son.'[2] The worship finally evoked by the events of the Gospel is neither a cult of Jesus nor a reformed prophetic Judaism with the Fatherhood in a new prominence, but the adoration of the triune God.

Incarnation

'The Word became flesh and dwelt among us; and we beheld his glory.' Not all who saw Jesus saw the glory, but only those with faith to discern it. From the rest it was hidden. If the rulers of the world had known it, 'they would not have crucified the Lord of glory' (1 Cor. ii, 8).

It was in humiliation that the glory was revealed on earth. There was the humiliation whereby the eternal Word took upon Himself the particularity of historical existence with all the limita-

---

[1] L. Hodgson: *The Doctrine of the Trinity*, p. 68.
[2] Eugène Masure: *The Christian Sacrifice*, p. 114.

tions which that particularity involved. There was the humiliation involved in the 'messianic secret' which the Synoptists describe: for Jesus could not express His messianic claims outright to all and sundry without the continual danger of the distortion of claims which no human language and no contemporary categories sufficed to convey. There was the humiliation whereby His mission was completed only in suffering and death. But if this threefold humiliation was, viewed from one angle, a concealment of the glory, it was, viewed from another angle, only an aspect of the glory. That the Son of God could thus make His own the frustrations of human life and death was a signal manifestation of the glory of the divine self-giving.[1] The mission of the Lord was at once the descent of one who trod the road of frustration, ignorance, pain and death and the ascent of one who was realizing in humiliation a glory which had been His from all eternity.

This paradox of the Incarnation is apparent in the Johannine language. On the one hand the Son retains on earth the glory which He ever had with the Father: 'the heavenly Word proceeding forth, yet leaving not the Father's side.' On the other hand the Son prays that the Father will bestow glory upon Him in the Passion and in the exaltation which will follow. There has been no abandonment of glory: yet the Son prays for glory and awaits the day when He will receive it. The right solution of this problem of Johannine exegesis seems to be that it is in His *human nature* that the Son receives glory from the Father, and He asks that through the Passion and Resurrection the human nature may be exalted into the eternal glory of the Godhead. Yet these

[1] This point, which is independent of formal doctrines of Kenosis, has been made both by ancient and modern writers. Thus Gregory of Nyssa: 'That the omnipotence of the Divine nature should have had strength to descend to the lowliness of humanity, furnishes a more manifest proof of power than even the greatness and supernatural character of the miracles.... It is not the vastness of the heavens and the bright shining of the constellations, the order of the universe and the administration over all existence that so manifestly displays the transcendent power of the Deity, as this condescension to the weakness of our nature,—the way in which sublimity is actually seen in lowliness, and yet the loftiness descends not.'—*Oratio Catechetica Magna*, xxiv. Cf. P. T. Forsyth: *The Person and Place of Jesus Christ*, chs. XI, XII, for a powerful modern exposition of a similar line of thought.

two data—the Son's abiding glory, the Son's reception of glory through death and resurrection—are as two facets of a single mystery. It is by the humiliation of the Son's winning of glory in the toils of history that the eternal glory of the divine self-giving is most signally disclosed.

Such is the glory of the Incarnate life. We read of it in the narratives of the ministry and the Passion. But behind it is the glory of the act of Incarnation itself. *Verbum caro factum*: it is not only in the story of the Incarnate Lord but in the fact that He became Incarnate that the glory is made known, evoking the worship of angels and men. 'The Christian, then, looks out upon a metaphysical landscape of almost unbearable grandeur which compels him to awestruck adoration. But within that landscape, bathed in the light of charity, he sees in its full and touching beauty the specific object of his worship. This specific object is not simply the human figure of the Incarnate, the 'historic Jesus', but the Eternal Godhead who here utters His word within the human arena and stoops to the human level; and whose inmost nature that figure reveals to men. . . . The real splendour of catholic devotion, its mingling of spaciousness and transcendence with homely love, is missed unless there is a remembrance of that unconditioned glory which enters our conditioned world through that lowly door.'[1]

Atonement

It might be thought that the conception of glory, linked as it is with the Incarnation, had less to do with the doctrine of Atonement. But closer study shews that the glory not only provides a pattern of the doctrine of Atonement but illuminates the inner unity of some aspects of that doctrine which have been too often separated.

Primarily and obviously glory suggests that aspect of the Atonement which is described in the phrase *Christus Victor*. The glory shewn forth on Calvary was a kingly power mightier than the human and cosmic evil which was ranged against it. The prince of this world was defeated and judged: the world was overcome. But the *Christus Victor* doctrine does not stand alone:

[1] Evelyn Underhill: *Christian Worship*, pp. 66-7.

it includes, in the Fourth Gospel, the doctrine of a godward offering whereby sin is expiated. The Passion is a glorifying of the Father inasmuch as it is the laying down of the Son's life as a sacrificial offering (cf. vi, 51; x, 18). The prayer for glory is also the prayer for Christ's self-consecration as a victim on behalf of the disciples (xvii, 1, 19). Hence in the story of the Passion the imagery of the victorious king who reigns from the tree is blended with the imagery of the sacrificial victim who expiates sin and brings communion between God and man, slain as he is at the passover time (xix, 14) and slain as a peace-offering without the breaking of a bone (xix, 36). The victory and the expiation are inseparable, and the δόξα expresses this. The δόξα is the utter self-giving of Christ to the Father which, released by His death and brought into touch with human lives by His Spirit, can become the new principle of self-giving within them and can banish from them the old principle of self-centred selfishness. Just as in Hebrews the sacrifice of Christ, through the sprinkling of the blood or sacrificial self-giving upon the consciences of men, breaks the power of sin, so in Saint John the glory of Christ's self-giving breaks the power of men's sinful glory of self-esteem. Christ's godward sacrifice for sin, Christ's victory over sin, Christ's sanctification of men by the Spirit: these aspects of Atonement are held together within the doctrine of the glory.

Church

'And the glory which thou hast given me, I have given unto them; that they may be one, even as we are one' (John xvii, 22). Herein lies the meaning of the Church. It is the mystery of the participation of men and women in the glory which is Christ's. Baptised into His death and made sharers in His resurrection they are members of the Body which is Christ's, branches of the vine who is Christ. Here the Spirit glorifies *Christ*, taking the things that are Christ's and declaring them to men (John xvi, 14). Here the *Father* is glorified by the fruitfulness of the disciples (John xv, 8). Here too *men* are glorified, even as they are called and justified (Rom. viii, 30). Here they are being transformed into Christ's image from glory to glory as from a sovereign Spirit (2 Cor. iii, 18). But beneath every act in the

Church whereby this many-sided work of glory is being wrought there is the truth about the Church's essential being, namely that the glory of Christ *is there*. The glory which Christians are to grow into and to manifest by the practical response of the Christian life is a glory which *is theirs* already.

Inasmuch as the glory dwells in it, the Church is the temple of God. In the post-exilic temple built by Zerubbabel and in the later temple built by Herod the glory had not returned. But now Christ's people, coming to Him 'a living stone, rejected indeed of men, but with God elect, precious', are built up 'as God's true temple' (1 Pet. ii, 4-5).[1] 'Know ye not', says Saint Paul, 'that ye are the temple of God, and that the Spirit of God dwelleth in you? If any man defile the temple of God, him shall God destroy; for the temple of God is holy, which temple ye are' (1 Cor. iii, 16-17). Again, 'what agreement hath the temple of God with idols? For ye are the temple of the living God; as God hath said, I will dwell in them, and walk in them; and I will be their God, and they shall be my people' (2 Cor. vi, 16). The Christians are 'an holy temple unto the Lord: in whom ye also are builded together for an habitation of God through the Spirit' (Eph. ii, 21-22).

Yet the knowledge that the glory dwells already in the Church may betray its members into the ancient sin whereby Israel ascribed the glory to itself, unless they are mindful of two warning truths of the apostolic teaching. (1) The first of these truths is that the glory in the church is an invisible glory. Though the Church is visible the glory is not to be confused with earthly majesty and splendour, for it is a glory discernible without and realized within—only through faith. It is hidden from the eyes of the unbelieving world and can never be displayed for that world's admiration; and it is hidden also from the members of the Church and can never be enjoyed by them in a quasi-worldly manner. 'Ye died, and your life is hid with Christ in God' (Col. iii, 3). Only at the Parousia will the glory become visible, and meanwhile 'neque Christum, neque Christianos novit mundus; ac ne Christiani quidem plane seipsos.'[2] (2) The second of these

---

[1] The reasons for this translation of οἶκος πνευματικός are stated by E. G. Selwyn: *The First Epistle of Saint Peter*, pp. 281-9.

[2] Bengel: *Gnomon Novi Testamenti*, on Col. iii, 1-4.

truths is that the glory in the Church is but a foretaste of the glory that is to come, and therefore the Church's sense of possession is mingled with the Church's sense of incompleteness. *Here* the powers of the age to come are at work within the Church's humiliation: *there* the open vision of a glory awaits the Church in the day when judgment will begin at the house of God. It follows that the Church's claims are ratified by the Church's humility, and the Church's riches by the Church's hunger for what she lacks. Torn from this eschatological context the doctrine of the Church becomes the doctrine of an institution among other institutions upon the plane of history. Set in this eschatological context it is the doctrine of a Church filled already with glory, yet humbled by the command to await both a glory and a judgment hereafter.

Eschatology

Throughout the investigation of the glory it has again and again been apparent that the 'last things' are not a far-off outwork of the structure of the Christian faith, but a determining factor within the structure. If there is already 'salvation', 'redemption', 'life', 'glory', it is so only because, through the agency of the Holy Spirit, an anticipation has been given to us of 'salvation', 'redemption', 'life', 'glory' that belong to the age to come. Of the powers of that age we have been allowed to taste.

The idea of the 'last things' has often been presented in terms of the destiny of the individual: 'what happens to me when I die?' But the Christian doctrine sees the destiny of the individual as one part of the pattern of the divine design for mankind and for all creation. God, who created the world for His glory, will glorify His creatures and lead them to glorify Him. The end is a new creation, forged from out of the broken pieces of a fallen creation, filled with glory and giving glory to its maker.

The crown of God's creation is man, made in the Creator's own image and possessing an affinity to Him in virtue of which he may come to know Him, to obey Him, to love Him and in the end to see Him. The service of God in the reflection of God's holiness and love is subsumed in the worship of God: and both the worship and the service are subsumed finally in the seeing of

GLORY AND TRANSFIGURATION

God as He is. The seeing of God amid the shadows of history in the Incarnate Life of the Son is far less than the seeing of God which will be 'face to face' (1 Cor. xiii, 12) and 'as he is' (1 John iii, 2). And this perfect seeing awaits the transforming of mankind into the image of Christ and their being made 'like Him.'

But besides his affinity to the Creator, in whose image he is made and to whose vision he strives to attain, Man has his place in relation to the rest of creation. He is set to rule over it as God's vicegerent, 'crowned with glory and honour' and with all things put in subjection under his feet (Ps. viii, 3–8); and in his worship of God he is the spokesman of all created things. The mystery of evil afflicts not man alone, but all creation too. The sufferings of men at this present time (Rom. viii, 18), the bondage of corruption in nature (Rom. viii, 21), the fact that we see not yet all things made subject to man (Heb. ii, 8), all betoken the frustration of the divine design by the fall. But by the Cross and Resurrection of Christ the inauguration of a new creation has begun, and this new creation will include both mankind brought to sonship and to glory (Rom. viii, 21; Heb. ii, 10), and nature renewed in union with man in the worship and praise of God (Rom. viii, 21). The Christian hope is therefore far more than the salvaging of human souls into a spiritual salvation: it is the re-creation of the world, through the power of the Resurrection of Christ.

Thus the hope of the beatific vision is crossed by the hope of the vindication of the divine design not only in man but in all things. And the hope of the resurrection of the body, when the body of our low estate is transformed into the body of Christ's glory (Phil. iii, 21), is the reminder of our kinship with the created world which the God of glory will redeem in a new world wherein the old is not lost but fulfilled.

CHAPTER IX

THE PRAISE OF HIS GLORY

THROUGHOUT THE whole of our study of the revelation of the Glory of God there has frequently come into view the complementary conception of the glorifying of God by man; and this conception now demands investigation. Δόξα as the glory has its counterpart in δόξα as praise and worship and in δοξάζειν as the verb which expresses this. God has declared His glory to the end that all creation may give glory to Him.¹

I

In the Old Testament man's duty of worship is inherent in his nature as man. Because he is made in God's image, after God's likeness, he has an affinity to God which requires that he make his boast in God and not in himself. But the meaning of man's worship is bound up with his place in the creation. He is set over the rest of God's created works as God's vicegerent, and in his praises of God he is creation's spokesman. Creation becomes articulate in and through man.²

Thwarted in his destiny as a worshipper by the sin of pride, man cannot worship unless his creator also be his redeemer. In the call and deliverance of Israel the divine redemption begins. In Israel man learns to worship: and the worship is characterized by homage to Yahveh as king, gratitude to Yahveh as deliverer, awe before the terrible signs of Yahveh's presence, and contrition before Yahveh's righteousness. But within Israel's worship

¹ Δοξάζειν in classical Greek has two meanings, corresponding to the normal meanings of the noun, (*a*) to think, to believe, to mean (eine Meinung haben); (*b*) to praise, to honour (Ruhm geben). In the LXX the first meaning disappears, and the second is frequent in reference both to praising men and to praising God. The same is true of the N.T.: an instance of the glorifying of *men* by others in Matt. vi, 2.

² L. S. Thornton: *The Common Life in the Body of Christ*, p. 358.

GLORY AND TRANSFIGURATION

of Israel's redeemer the sense of man's adoration of man's creator is not left behind but rather fulfilled and released. It is as if creation finds its voice in man, and man's lips are unsealed in Israel to tell the praises of the God who is both the maker of all things and the king of His people. The Psalter gives utterance to a worship in which man's sense of awe and wonder at the greatness and goodness of his maker and saviour are deepened by his sense of lowly creatureliness as he leads the praises of created things: 'all thy works shall give thanks unto thee, O Lord; and thy saints shall bless thee. They shall speak of the glory of thy kingdom, and talk of thy power' (Ps. cxlv, 10–11).

The most significant of the Old Testament words in this connection is not *halel*, to 'glory' in the sense of to 'boast' (cf. Jer. ix, 24: 'let him that glorieth glory in the LORD'), but *kabed*, to 'glorify' in the sense of to render *kabod* or glory. The different uses of *kabed* throw some light upon the Biblical conception of worship. Thus we find (1) *kabed*, used actively, to glorify God (Ps. xxii, 23; l, 15; l, 23; lxxxvi, 9, 12; Isa. xxiv, 15; xxv, 3; (2) *kabed*, used passively, God is or will be glorified (Lev. x, 3; Isa. xxvi, 15; Ezek. xxviii, 22; xxxix, 13; Hag. i, 8); (3) *kabod* the noun, used of glory given to God (Jos. vii, 19; 1 Sam. vi, 5; 1 Chron. xvi, 29; Jer. xiii, 16; Mal. ii, 2; Ps. xxix, 1–2; xcvi, 7–8; cxv, 1). But besides the *giving* of glory of God there are the kindred phrases: to *declare* it (1 Chron. xvi, 24; Ps. xcvi, 3); to *speak* of it (Ps. cxlv, 11); to *sing* of it (Ps. cxxxviii, 5); to *let it be* over the earth (Ps. lvii, 5, cf. Ps. lxxii, 19). This analysis of language tells its own tale. When men glorify Yahveh they do not add to His glory. They acknowledge it, submit to it, set their affections upon it, seek its greater manifestation, pray and give praise for it. And, since the glory of Yahveh in His purpose in history is clouded by Israel's sinfulness, Israel can give glory to Him aright and set forth His glory among the nations only if Israel is herself a people in whose conduct He is glorified. The recurring insistence of the prophet Ezekiel that Yahveh demands to be glorified in a cleansed and righteous Israel is the key to the hope of the recognition of Yahveh's glory throughout the human race. Israel glorifying God involves the glory of God, in the fullness of its ethical meaning, dwelling in Israel.

It is not the task of this book to trace the story, with its constant tensions, between priest and prophet, between cultus and ethics, between Yahveh's tabernacling presence and Yahveh's judgment of the nation, between Israel's privilege and Israel's missionary duty. The principles could not be carried out within the bounds of the old covenant; and Israel, as she learned more and more about the offering which God requires, discovered more and more her impotence to offer it. Her scriptures and her institutions pointed forward to an act of glory and a response of glorifying beyond the power of sinful man. In Christ there is both the final utterance of the Yea of the divine glory, and the perfect response of the Amen of Man's glorifying of God.

2

The perfect act of worship is seen only in the Son of Man. By Him alone there is made the perfect acknowledgment upon earth of the glory of God and the perfect response to it. On the one hand the prophetic revelation of the glory of God is summed up in Him as He is Himself the glory of which the prophets, all unknowing, spake (cf. John xii, 41). On the other hand the ancient sacrifices are fulfilled in Him as He, priest and victim, makes the rational offering of His will in Gethsemane and on the Cross. In Christ the praise of God, the wonder before God, the thirst for God, the zeal for God's righteousness, which fill the pages of the Psalter, find pure and flawless utterance. And in Him too man's contrition for his own sin and the sin of the race finds its perfect expression; for the sinless Christ made before God that perfect acknowledgment of man's sin which man cannot make for himself.

Without speaking of a glorifying of the Father by the Son the Synoptic Gospels lay bare the elements wherein the glorifying consists. As a boy in the temple Jesus puts first 'the Father's business' (Luke ii, 49). At the baptism in Jordan Jesus makes Himself one with the penitence of sinful men (Mark i, 5, 9). At every crisis in His ministry Jesus seeks the face of the Father in prayer (Luke iii, 21; vi, 12; ix, 18, 28; xi, 1; xxii, 32, 41; xxiii, 46). He exults in the Holy Spirit because the mysteries of the Gospel have been revealed to babes (Luke x, 21), and he weeps over the unresponsiveness of Jerusalem (Luke xix, 41). The sayings of

GLORY AND TRANSFIGURATION

Jesus shew again and again the conviction of the Father's sovereignty, in all things: in nature, in history, and in the sufferings which He accepts as a cup from the Father's hand. And finally, in the certainty of the Father's sovereignty, there is the obedience to His will in the garden of Gethsemane and in the desolation of the hours upon Calvary. If all is summed up in the voice at the Baptism 'my son, the beloved in whom I have found satisfaction', it is summed up no less truly in the Johannine language: the Son glorifies the Father.

Risen and ascended the Son for ever glorifies the Father; and in this glorifying (which was from all eternity) the human nature, assumed in the Incarnation, now shares. The Johannine doctrine of the glorifying assists our understanding of the conception in the Epistle to the Hebrews of Christ as our great highpriest. Christ's priesthood belongs, as does His sonship, to the eternal world: for ever Son, He is also for ever priest. Priesthood means offering, and in the Son there is for ever that spirit of self-offering which the sacrifice of Calvary uniquely disclosed in our world of sin and death. The sacrifice of Calvary has been wrought once for all; but now Christ as high-priest 'ever liveth to make intercession' for 'them that draw near unto God through him' (Heb. vii, 25), and has entered 'into heaven itself, now to appear before the face of God for us' (Heb. ix, 24). Though Calvary can never be repeated, Christ is for ever with the Father in that character of self-giving and self-offering of which Calvary was the decisive historical utterance. In the ascended Christ there exists our human nature rendering to the Father the glory which Man was created in order to render; and, whether we speak of this as the presence of our high-priest before the Father's face or as the glorifying of the Father by the Son who was made man and died for us, the essential meaning is the same.

In union with its heavenly Lord the Church on earth worships, looking back to what He did once on Calvary and looking up to what He now is with the Father. It is a worship in Christ and through Christ. If it be called a worship of sacrificial offering, it is so because it is through Christ who is high-priest: 'through him thou let us offer up a sacrifice of praise to God continually, that is, the fruit of lips which make confession to his name' (Heb. xiii, 15). If it be called a worship of glorifying, it is so because it is through Christ who glorifies the Father: 'wherefore also through him is the Amen, unto the glory of God through us' (2 Cor. i, 20).

3

The response of worship begins during the earthly ministry of our Lord. Saint Mark most frequently describes the attitude of the people as awe and astonishment; but Saint Matthew mentions acts of reverential worship, the word used being προσκυνεῖν (Matt. viii, 2; ix, 18; xiv, 33; xv, 25; xx, 20; xxviii, 9, 17). Only rarely do these two evangelists say that the people 'glorified' God (Mark ii, 12; Matt. ix, 8; xv, 31). Saint Luke on the other hand more often uses δόξα, δοξάζειν to describe the people's reaction to the gracious acts and words of the Messiah. The shepherds (Luke ii, 20), the people in Galilee (iv, 15), the palsied man (v, 25), the eye-witnesses of the miracle at Nain (vii, 16), the woman with a spirit of infirmity (xiii, 13), the Samaritan leper (xvii, 15), the blind man (xviii, 43), the crowd at the triumphal entry (xix, 38), the centurion on Calvary (xxiii, 47) are all said to *glorify* God; and the apostles after the Ascension are said to bless him (εὐλογεῖν). It is possible that Saint Luke may be in some degree reading back into the life of Jesus the atmosphere of worship which belonged to the Church after the Resurrection.

It is after the Resurrection and Pentecost that the lips of the new Israel are unsealed to give glory to God in the fullness of the truth of the new covenant. The spread of the gospel and the common life of the Church are accompanied by strains of doxology. Thus in Acts:

1. The people glorify God upon the healing of the man at the beautiful gate (iv, 21). This is in line with the instances in Saint Luke's Gospel.
2. The Church in Jerusalem glorifies God on the news of the extension of the Gospel to Gentiles at Caesarea (xi, 18).
3. Gentiles at Antioch in Pisidia glorify God (xiii, 48).
4. The brethren in Jerusalem glorify God on Saint Paul's arrival (xxi, 20).

In the Epistles we read:

1. The apostles in Jerusalem glorified God 'in' Saint Paul, acknowledging his conversion and apostleship (Gal. i, 24).

GLORY AND TRANSFIGURATION

2. Christians must glorify God in their bodies (1 Cor. vi, 20).
3. They must do all to the glory of God (1 Cor. x, 31).
4. The collection for the poor in Jerusalem is for the glory of God (2 Cor. ix, 13).
5. The Church in Rome will glorify God (Rom. xv, 6); and the end of Saint Paul's apostleship is that the Gentiles will glorify Him (Rom. xv, 9).
6. The righteousness of Christians is for the glorifying of God (Phil. i, 11).
7. So are their sufferings, amid which the glory rests upon them (1 Pet. iv, 16, cf. John xxi, 19: 'this he said, signifying by what death he should glorify God').
8. Prayer is asked 'that the word of the Lord may run and be glorified' (2 Thess. iii, 1).
9. The mystery of God's redemption is wrought with the praise of the glory of God as its goal (Eph. i, 6, 12, 14).

So it is that a spirit of doxology fills the early Christians amid all that they do and suffer, and the great formal Doxologies are its summaries. In these the praise and thankfulness which accompany every aspect of the daily life of the Church are consciously related to the great doctrines of God as creator and saviour. Each of the Doxologies dwells upon some aspect of the name or the work of God.

1. His inscrutable wisdom in the operations of His sovereign purpose (Rom. xi, 33–6).
2. His power to stablish men in the Gospel which fulfils the age-long purpose of 'the only wise God' (Rom. xvi, 25–7).
3. His deliverance of us from this evil world by the Cross (Gal. i, 4–5).
4. His power at work within the Church (Eph. iii, 20–1).
5. His eternal, incorruptible, invisible being (1 Tim. i, 17).
6. His promise of deliverance into the heavenly kingdom (2 Tim. iv, 18).
7. His grace working through the risen Jesus as shepherd of the sheep (Heb. xiii, 20–1).
8. His sovereignty in a time of suffering. (1 Pet. iv, 11).
9. His power to preserve His people and to bring them into the presence of His glory (Jud. 24–5).

Finally, in the doxologies of the Apocalypse, God is glorified in the whole drama of His righteous acts as creator, redeemer and judge.

Unto him that loveth us, and loosed us from our sins by his blood; and he made us to be a kingdom, to be priests unto his God and Father; to him be the glory and the dominion for ever and ever. Amen (Rev. i, 6).

And every created thing which is in heaven, and on the earth, and under the earth, and on the sea, and all things that are in them, heard I saying, Unto him that sitteth on the throne and unto the lamb, be the blessing and the honour and the glory and the dominion, for ever and ever (Rev. v, 13).

Who shall not fear, O Lord, and glorify thy name? for thou only art holy; for all the nations shall come and worship before thee; for thy righteous acts have been made manifest. (Rev. xv, 4.)

4

In spite of the utter newness of the access to the Father through Jesus in one Spirit which the new covenant has brought, the worship of the new ecclesia has a real continuity with the worship of the old. It is the same God of glory who is worshipped. His glory in the overthrowing of Pharaoh and in the leading of Israel through the Red Sea has its counterpart in His glory in Christ's victory over sin and death and in the exodus of the new Israel in Jerusalem. His glory in the creation is not forgotten but enhanced in the worship of Him as redeemer. In a truly catholic worship the joyful access of Christians to a Father and the thankfulness of Christians to a Saviour are interpenetrated by the adoration offered by the creature to the Creator. Herein is the blending of action and passivity, of movement and rest, which belongs to the tradition of the worship of the Catholic Church.

Within the new ecclesia the scriptures of the old ecclesia are retained as Holy Scriptures, for they are now seen to speak of Christ and His glory. Among these scriptures the Psalter has its special place. The Psalter is used in the Church not as the expression of individual mood or feeling but with a twofold rationale. (1) It is the voice of the Israel of God, worshipping now as of old the creator, king and redeemer and praying for victory over its enemies which are no less deadly because they are spiritual, subtle and unseen. (2) It is the prayer book of Christ Himself. In His own use of them its words of adoration, supplication and self-committal were brought to their perfect end. Using the Psalter in the name of Christ the members of the Body make their own the prayer of the Head.

At the heart of the Church's glorifying of God there is however the new rite of the Eucharist. Here the Church is united to the glory of Christ on Calvary and in heaven, and finds the focus of the glorifying of God by all created things.

In the upper room our Lord (i) gave thanks to God over the loaf at the beginning of the supper and over the cup at the end of the supper ($\epsilon\dot{v}\chi\alpha\rho\iota\sigma\tau\dot{\eta}\sigma\alpha s$), (ii) identified the loaf with His body and the wine with His blood—that is with His life surrendered in sacrificial offering, (iii) bade His disciples partake of both the body and the blood, (iv) predicted a feasting with them in the messianic age. This eucharistic action may be interpreted by the language of the Fourth Gospel. Inasmuch as our Lord, by His actions and words with the loaf and the cup, is declaring Himself to be dedicated to a sacrificial death, He is indeed glorifying the Father (John xvii, 1) and consecrating Himself on behalf of the disciples (John xvii, 19). Inasmuch as He bids the disciples to feed upon His life surrendered as a sacrifice it is here that 'the glory which thou gavest me I have given unto them' (John xvii, 22). The food which they receive is the life of Christ laid down in godward offering: the glory which they are given is the glory wherewith Christ glorified the Father.

Thus the subsequent eucharistic worship of the Church is on its godward side a participation in Christ's glorifying of the Father, and on its manward side a receiving of Christ's glory— the glory of the Cross. Inasmuch as the rite is a shewing-forth of Christ's death (1 Cor. xi, 26) it recalls the glory of Calvary. Inasmuch as it is a sharing in the body of Christ and in the blood of Christ (1 Cor. x, 16) it unites those who partake with the glory of Christ as He now is—risen, ascended and glorifying the Father. Inasmuch as it employs God's common gifts of bread and wine and brings them to be blessed, it is a glorifying of the Creator by the giving back of His own created gifts to Him. And inasmuch as it points forward to the coming of Christ again (1 Cor. xi, 26) it is an anticipation of that feasting with Christ in the world to come, when Him whom we now perceive by faith we shall behold with open face.

Inasmuch as the glory is the glory of Father and Son in the bond of love, the eucharistic gift of glory to the disciples is tested in their unity. The Pauline 'we being many are one bread, one body, for we all partake of the one bread' is tested in the Johannine, 'the glory which thou hast given me I have given unto them; that they may be one, even as we are one' (John xvii, 22). The new covenant in the blood of Christ is inseparable from the new commandment of mutual love in the manifestation of Christ's own love (John xiii, 31–5). Hence the common life of the Christian fellowship is not only a witness to the glory, but is itself the glory of the Father and the Son shewn forth to the world. Without this common life—*ichabod*, the glory is departed.

5

The godward life of the Church includes the manward mission of the Church, not merely as a close corollary but as a very part of that life. Christ's own proclamation of the word to the disciples (John xvii, 6) was a part of His glorifying of the Father (John xvii, 4); and the disciples' own ministry of the word (John xvii, 20) is the means whereby men are led to share in the glory (John xvii, 22). Saint Paul likewise after describing the Christians as beholding the glory and being transformed into it from glory unto glory (2 Cor. iii, 17) goes on to tell of the preaching by the apostles of the gospel of the glory of Christ (2 Cor. iv, 3–6).

The preaching of the glory of Christ, if it is guided by the New Testament use of δόξα, has as its centre the Resurrection with the Cross as its prelude, and it leads men to see the significance of the ministry and teaching of our Lord with the light of Calvary and Easter upon it. The preaching will appeal to the affinity between the gospel and mankind as created in the divine image, and its preachers will commend themselves 'to every man's conscience in the sight of God' (2 Cor. iv, 2). But the warning of Saint Paul must be heeded: 'But and if our gospel is veiled, it is veiled in them that are perishing: in whom the god of this world hath blinded the minds of the unbelieving, that the light of the gospel of the glory of Christ who is the image of God, should not dawn upon them' (2 Cor. iv, 3-4). It is not to be thought that the gospel will be made simple to the worldly and the impenitent, and the attempt to make it simple to them may corrupt or distort it.

For, as has been wisely said:[1] 'the simplicity of the gospel lies in the simplicity of the moral issues which it raises, and not in the ease with which its teaching can be explained to the careless and the hardened.' The injunction to let our light so shine before men that they may see our good works and so be led to glorify God (Matt. v, 16) does not mean that a programme of good works can commend the gospel by meeting men's ideals upon their own level, without any challenge to the assumptions on which those ideals often rest. The fellowship of the Church can indeed manifest the glory of God to the consciences of men; but it does so not by providing something for impenitent men to like and admire, but by being a fellowship so filled with God Himself that the conscience is pierced by God's love and judgment. Thus the Gospel of the Glory of God is always very near to mankind, and yet always very far from them: near, because the divine image is in mankind and the Gospel is the true meaning of man; far, because it is heard only by a faith and a repentance which overthrow all man's glorying in himself and his works.

> And I saw another angel flying in mid heaven, having an eternal Gospel to proclaim unto them that dwell on the earth, and unto every nation and tribe and tongue and people; and he saith with a great voice, Fear God, and give him glory; for the hour of his judgment is come: and worship him that made the heaven and the earth and sea and fountains of waters (Rev. xiv, 6-7).

[1] H. L. Goudge: *The Second Epistle to the Corinthians*, p. 39, in a most illuminating discussion of this problem.

PART II:
THE TRANSFIGURATION OF CHRIST

CHAPTER X

THE STUDY OF THE TRANSFIGURATION

I

THE FIRST three evangelists describe an occasion in which our Lord, in the midst of His earthly ministry, was seen by three disciples in His heavenly glory. The familiar English title of the event, the Transfiguration, has come from the word used in Saint Mark and Saint Matthew, μετεμορφώθη, *transfiguratus est*. But its significance is perhaps better expressed in the German title, *die Verklärung*, the glorification; for though Saint Luke's narrative alone contains the word 'glory' the word summarizes the dominant idea of all the narratives.

Jesus leads Peter, James and John to a high mountain, where they see Him transformed in an intense blaze of light. Moses and Elijah appear in converse with Him; and finally a cloud envelopes Him and a voice is heard: 'this is my Son, the chosen: hear ye him.' The light and the cloud connect the episode plainly with the subject of the first part of this book, even without the explicit statement of Saint Luke, 'they saw his glory'. Further, the place of the story in the narratives (particularly in that of Saint Mark) enhances its importance. Leading up to it there is the confession of Saint Peter, the first prediction of the Passion, the summons to the would-be disciples to take up their crosses and follow Jesus, the prediction of the coming of the Son of Man in the glory of the Father. Beyond it there is the journey to Jerusalem and the story of the Passion. Thus the Transfiguration seems to stand at a watershed in the ministry of Jesus, and to be a height from which the reader looks down on one side upon the Galilean ministry and on the other side upon the *Via Crucis*. The story resembles the Baptism of Jesus, inasmuch as it culminates in a heavenly voice proclaiming the Sonship; and it resembles the agony in Gethsemane, inasmuch as it shews the three disciples witnessing a decisive moment in the relation of Jesus to the Father.

The modern study of the Transfiguration has passed through phases determined by the general tendencies of New Testament criticism. There was the period of the liberal 'Lives of Jesus' based especially upon the narrative of Saint Mark. In some of these 'lives' the Transfiguration was rationalized or explained away or regarded as an unhistorical accretion in accordance with a general rejection of the supernatural element in the Gospel narratives. In other of these 'lives' the Transfiguration was retained as an important episode in the story, and treated in connection with the psychology of our Lord and the disciples and expounded as a supreme 'spiritual experience' or crisis in the inner life of our Lord and in the training of the twelve. This method of treatment produced some writing of much beauty and reverence, but it involved a reading of the Gospel narratives more biographical and psychological than the character of the narratives warrants. Later there came the work of the critics who questioned the historical character of Mark, and ascribed its messianic elements to a tendentious reading-back of the post-Resurrection faith of the Church. Thus Wellhausen held that the Transfiguration-story had its origin in a post-Resurrection appearance of Jesus, and a host of commentators followed him in this view. Meanwhile the historical character of the narrative found defenders in terms of the experience of Christian mysticism; and in this connection Miss Evelyn Underhill's *The Mystic Way* had no small influence. More recently under the influence of Form-criticism there has been a sustained attempt to relate the story of the Transfiguration to theological traditions and motifs within the thought of the early Church.

It is within the last category that the most considerable recent studies of the Transfiguration fall. Ernst Lohmeyer's article, 'Die Verklärung Jesu nach dem Markus-Evangelium', was published in 1922.[1] Here Lohmeyer traced Saint Mark's narrative of the Transfiguration to two separate traditions: a Jewish-Christian tradition of the witness of Elijah and Moses to the Messiahship of Jesus, and an Hellenistic-Christian tradition of a metamorphosis whereby the heavenly Son of God is manifested on earth.

[1] See *Zeitschrift für Neutestamentliche Wissenschaft*, 1922, pp. 185-245.

But this part of Lohmeyer's thesis was perhaps the least important, for he seems in his commentary on Saint Mark, published in 1937,[1] to have abandoned it in favour of the view that the story is a unity. More significant therefore is that part of his thesis in which he discusses the theological background of the *phenomena* of the Transfiguration story, particularly the significance of Moses and Elijah and of the tabernacles mentioned in Saint Peter's interjection. All these he finds to be *eschatological* in their symbolism: the coming of Moses and Elijah portends the nearness of the end of the age, and the reference to tabernacles has as its background the eschatological associations of the Feast of Tabernacles in connection with the idea of the tabernacling of God with his people. G. H. Boobyer elaborated some of Lohmeyer's points in his *Saint Mark and the Transfiguration Story*, 1940. Boobyer's work is the most thorough monograph on the Transfiguration which has appeared in English, and he has put students of the subject greatly in his debt. Though some of his points do not carry conviction, he seems to the present writer to make good his main thesis—that Saint Mark regarded the Transfiguration as a foretaste of the glory of Jesus at the Parousia. Far less valuable is the most recent of all works on the subject, Harald Riesenfeld's *Jésus Transfiguré*, published in Copenhagen in 1947. Here the search for theological motifs is carried to lengths which are somewhat fanciful. Following Mowinckel's theory of an annual feast of the enthroning of Yahveh in Israel, Riesenfeld goes on to find a conception of the enthroning of the Messiah to be prominent in the Jewish messianic hope, and he believes that this conception underlies much of the New Testament idea of Messiahship and in particular the traditions of the Transfiguration. In the course of his argument conjecture frequently does duty for proof, and the long chain of conjectures is no stronger than its weakest links.[2]

[1] *Das Evangelium des Markus*, 1937, being a volume in Meyer's commentary.
[2] Riesenfeld's book came into my hands at a late stage in the preparation of this work, but I do not think an earlier acquaintance with his arguments would have modified my treatment. He makes some valuable criticisms of the extreme claim made by Boobyer on behalf of an eschatological interpretation of the Transfiguration, and he makes some interesting suggestions; but his thesis is vitiated by his application to the N.T. of unproved assumptions about the Jewish cultus and by his *complete* ignoring of the problem of history in connec-

GLORY AND TRANSFIGURATION

The problems and difficulties disclosed in these different phases of study have delayed the inclusion of the Transfiguration within the positive theological and historical treatment of the New Testament which is characteristic of the present day. It is noteworthy that some of the most important recent works upon the theology and history of the Gospels omit the Transfiguration altogether; and the episode tends to be in the hands either of those who treat the life of our Lord in a very conservative way, or of those who study theological motifs without regard to the question of history. Plainly it is relevant to inquire into the main ideas connected, in the Jewish mind and in the Christian Church, with Moses and Elijah, the tabernacles, the cloud and the heavenly voice. But just as the Christian conception of our Lord's Messiahship arose not from an amalgam of current notions but from a history which re-created them, so in particular the story of the Transfiguration may be the creation not of certain *theologumena* but of the creative history that moulded them.[1]

2

First among the critical questions which have been prominent is that of the post-Resurrection theory of the Transfiguration. Wellhausen, Loisy, Bultmann, Montefiore, Goguel and many other scholars have held this view; and it became almost a commonplace amongst advanced critics in the first three decades of this century.

In some of the expositions of this theory the strongest reason for it was simply an *a priori* feeling that an event of this sort is

tion with the narratives. He connects Hebrews i, 3-14, Revelation i, 12-17, v, 1-12, vii, 9-12, with the idea of the enthronization of the Messiah, the key thought in the Transfiguration. The shining raiment of the transfigured Jesus is connected with kingly robes, cf. the robes in which Jesus was mocked in the Passion. 'It is good for us to be here' links the Transfiguration with the idea of the Sabbath rest of the messianic age; cf. the messianic significance of the treatment of the Sabbath by our Lord. Pp. 1-240 deal with the background of Jewish cultus; pp. 243-306 with the narratives of the Transfiguration.

[1] To my great regret I have been unable to procure J. Holler: *Die Verklärung Jesu*, Freiburg 1937, and J. Blinzler: *Die Neutestamentlichen Berichte uber die Verklärung Jesu*, Münster 1937. Both are the work of Roman Catholic scholars, and were reviewed by J. M. Creed in *Journal of Theological Studies*, Oct. 1938.

THE STUDY OF THE TRANSFIGURATION

incongruous with the earthly ministry of Jesus. So Loisy: 'On a pu conjecturer avec assez de vraisemblance que la transfiguration avait été primitivement une apparition du Christ réssuscité, une vision de Pierre, et que l'indication des six jours était, à l'origine, en rapport avec la passion... le tableau, en effet n'a de sens que par rapport à la gloire du Christ réssuscité; il répond aux préoccupations de la communauté chrétienne, et n'aurait pas eu de signification pour les apôtres durant le ministère de Jésus.'[1] Thus Loisy put the event after the Resurrection because it seemed to him to be devoid of any meaning at an earlier stage. Wellhausen put the event after the Resurrection because, following Wrede, he held that it was not until then that the Messiahship of Jesus was proclaimed or believed. To him the Transfiguration story is based upon a post-Resurrection proclamation of the Sonship of Jesus (cf. Rom. i, 4) and upon an appearance to Peter (cf. I Cor. xv, 5). The theory is plainly linked to the presupposition that no events or sayings of an avowedly messianic character occurred during the earthly ministry of Jesus, and that records of such events or sayings are an importation from the post-Resurrection stage of the story.

The treatment of the question by some more recent writers using the methods of Form-criticism has been more scientific. It has been pointed out that, if Mark's gospel is not an ordered biography but a series of isolated episodes, the section Mark ix, 2-9 may be out of place where it stands, breaking as it seems the sequence of Mark ix, 1 and ix, 11ff. It would be easy for pre-Resurrection and post-Resurrection episodes in the tradition to be confused; and, if the core of this particular story was an appearance of Jesus to Peter, it is possible that the story became elaborated with significant 'theological' additions—the cloud, the voice, the heavenly witnesses. Further, in the second century Ethiopic work, *The Apocalypse of Peter*, there is a story—in a post-Resurrection setting—of Jesus appearing in glory with Moses and Elijah as witnesses: the heavenly voice is heard, the cloud appears, Jesus and the two witnesses are born away in the cloud, and the hosts of heaven greet them.[2]

[1] *Les Evangiles Synoptiques*, II, pp. 39-40.
[2] The text is given in M. R. James: *The Apocryphal New Testament*, pp. 510-21.

GLORY AND TRANSFIGURATION

The case is argued on these lines by K. G. Goetz in his book *Petrus* (pp. 76–89). But it has been subjected to devastating criticism by Boobyer (op. cit., pp. 11–16). He argues convincingly that the *Apocalypse of Peter* contains not a Resurrection-tradition so much as an Ascension story, built up from the traditions of the Transfiguration and suggesting that in the early Church the Transfiguration-imagery was connected with the Parousia. Above all, he shews that Goetz's theory is *mere* conjecture: a series of possibilities are made to do duty for an argument. It must also be noticed that the exponents of the post-Resurrection theory differ as to which are the original elements in the story and which are the later elaborations, and there is no core of the story which is agreed to bear indications of belonging to the post-Resurrection stage. Indeed the theory seems to be a very precarious alternative to the view that the event really happened, as Mark tells us, during the ministry of Jesus. It is noteworthy that in many commentators the theory is not argued so much as tacitly assumed as a critical position bequeathed from the era of Wrede and Wellhausen.

2

If then it is reasonable to believe that the tradition belongs originally to the period of the ministry of Jesus, of what sort was the event behind it? Was it an objective occurrence or a vision seen by one or all of the three disciples present?

The answer will turn in part upon our belief concerning the person of Jesus Christ. If the view of His person which was held by the evangelists and the apostolic Church in general is true, then a frankly supernatural occurrence in the course of His earthly ministry will be credible. None the less it is right to ask whether the supernatural occurrence had the nature of a 'vision' on the part of one or more of the disciples, and the study of the visionary experiences of Christian mysticism may be relevant.

It is known from the lives of the saints that an intense communion of the soul with God has brought to the body a supernatural radiance. In the lives of Saint Teresa, Saint Catherine of Bologna, Saint Catherine of Genoa and Saint Francis of Assisi such 'transfiguration' has been recorded: Miss Underhill has

THE STUDY OF THE TRANSFIGURATION

described it as 'one of the best attested of the abnormal phenomena connected with the mystic type'.[1] The most striking analogy is the story of Saint Francis, when he withdrew to Mount Alverna in the upper valley of the Arno for a season of prayer and communion with Christ's passion. In the presence of his four companions 'he was uplifted towards God in seraphic ardour of desire, and was transfigured into the likeness of Him who of His exceeding love was willing to be crucified', and the communion of his soul had bodily effects in the *stigmata* which remained with him until his death.[2] In her study of the bearing of those parallels upon the story of the Transfiguration Miss Underhill concluded that 'in the present state of the evidence a definite rejection of those narratives is as unscientific as the worst performances of pious credulity'. And if the Transfiguration was the outcome of the enwrapped communion of our Lord with His Father, then Saint Luke's description takes us near to what happened: 'as he was praying, the fashion of his countenance was altered, and his raiment became white and dazzling.'

Thus the Transfiguration itself may lie in the region not of a vision of the disciples but of a real occurrence in our Lord's soul and body. As for the accompanying details—Elijah with Moses, the cloud, the voice—these may lie in the region of mystic vision and audition. So Miss Underhill suggested that 'what they saw in Jesus was truly there for them to see, but for the rest they saw as in a vision'. The vision, while it was the vision of a truth which Jesus alone had revealed to them, drew upon the imagery which their own mind and tradition provided—the Old Testament figures, the Shekinah cloud, the voice. Thus the whole story contained both an objective occurrence in Jesus and a consequent vision on the part of the disciples, the latter depending upon the former and being created by it.

But what of Elijah and Moses? Miss Underhill put them simply within the disciples' vision, along with the cloud. But a more recent mystical writer, Miss Maisie Spens,[3] suggests that the converse between Jesus and the two heavenly figures belonged not to the disciples' vision but to the real experience of

---

[1] E. Underhill: *The Mystic Way*, p. 116.
[2] Cf. *The Legend of the Three Companions*, c. 69.
[3] In *Concerning Himself*, pp. 74-9.

Jesus that created it. Suggesting that there was a truly personal affinity between our Lord and those two men of God who had served God on earth in the past and were now alive unto God, she says: 'Mere "representativeness" is too abstract. . . . Moses and Elijah participated in the Transfiguration as their own individual selves, in virtue of their personal relation not to the body of the Law nor to the school of the prophets, but to Jesus Himself.'[1] In other words the disciples 'saw' Elijah and Moses only because their presence was already real to the soul and mind of Jesus. A similar view has been expressed by Dr. Lowther-Clarke: 'Whatever took place was primarily in our Lord's consciousness. We may suppose that the two great figures of God's people in the past were vividly present to Him . . . and that He communed with them in the spirit. For a brief space the disciples were able to enter into the Lord's consciousness and see with His eyes.'[2]

We are here in the realm of conjecture. There are limits to what the mystical and psychological studies of Miss Underhill and others can do for us. Their relevance has its limits—inasmuch as a supernatural event in the mission of the unique Son of God may have no parallel in the experiences of the saints. Their historical value has its limits—inasmuch as the gospels themselves are so innocent of psychological interests that it is hazardous to judge their testimony psychologically. Nevertheless these studies have not been a waste of time. The story of the Transfiguration with its marvellous blending of richness and simplicity is on any shewing the product of some creative mind and will. And we may not err in thinking that the creative mind and will resided not in the theologizing of the early Christian communities nor in the psychologizing of the disciples, but in the person of the Word-made-flesh at a crucial moment in His earthly life.

[1] Op. cit., p. 75. Miss Spens speaks of the 'life-affinity which our Lord sensed with Moses and Elijah', and in a passage of much beauty and restrained suggestiveness she draws out the nature of the affinity. 'The vocations of Moses and Elijah . . . in their striking analogies to His own, must have come as a mine of comfort and illumination.'

[2] W. K. Lowther-Clarke: *New Testament Problems*, p. 35.

THE STUDY OF THE TRANSFIGURATION

4

The *materials* of the Transfiguration story have, as we saw, been the subject of the most recent phase of study. What did the shining light, Moses and Elijah, the tabernacles, the cloud, the heavenly voice *mean* to a devout Jew or to an early Christian? Some of the symbols fall within the theme of the first part of the book, and already have had their explanation stated there; others are less obvious.

The *changed appearance of Jesus* ('his garments became glistering, exceeding white', Mark; 'his face shone as the sun', Matt.; 'the fashion of his countenance was altered and his raiment became white and dazzling', Luke) has clear affinity to the Apocalyptic ideas of the glory of the Messiah and the saints in heaven, and to Jesus's own predictions of the coming of the Son of Man in glory.

The *cloud* is familiar in the narratives of Exodus as the seat of the presence of the glory of God. Matthew emphasizes the connection by calling it a *shining* cloud ($\phi\omega\tau\epsilon\iota\nu\acute{\eta}$), a strictly accurate reference to the cloud with the light piercing it from within. Its appearance is expected at the end of the age (cf. 2 Macc. ii, 8). It seems hazardous to follow Boobyer in thinking that the cloud is here not the cloud at rest on earth, as in Exodus, but a moving cloud in which or on which the Messiah descends to earth at the Parousia (he compares Dan. vii, 13; 2 Bar. liii, 1-12; 4 Ezra xiii, 3).

What of *Moses and Elijah*? Here it is necessary to search out the relevant Jewish traditions.

The Apocalyptic books contain a good many references to the appearance of ancient heroes at the coming of the Messiah. Ezra (4 Ezra xiv, 9), Baruch (2 Bar. lxxvi, 2), Jeremiah (2 Macc. ii, 1) will have their place. And others besides: 'and ye shall see Enoch, Noah and Shem and Abraham and Isaac and Jacob rising at the right hand of gladness' (Test. Benj. x, 5-6). But a special interest attached to men who had, according to the scriptures, been translated so as never to die. Such were Enoch and Elijah: 'And they shall see the men that have been taken up, who have not tasted death from their birth; and the heart of the inhabitants shall be changed, and turned into another meaning' (2 Esdras vi, 26). It is within this conception that the explanation of the appearance of Moses and Elijah at the Transfiguration has been sought.

In the case of Elijah the evidence is very clear. He was believed to have been carried up into heaven (2 Kings ii, 11). And Malachi had predicted his return as the forerunner: 'Behold, I will send Elijah the prophet before the grea: and terrible day of the Lord come. And he shall turn the heart of the fathers to the children, and the heart of the children to their fathers, lest I come and smite the earth with a curse' (Mal. iv, 5-6). The belief that Elijah will precede the Messiah was common amongst our Lord's contemporaries (cf. Mark viii, 28; ix, 11; Matt. xi, 14; John i, 21). In the case of Moses however the traditions are less clear-cut. 'No one saw his grave' (Deut. xxxiv, 6), and later fancy built upon the idea that his death was in some way mysterious and held that he had a great role still to play in heaven. *The Assumption of Moses*, a work of the first century A.D., ascribes to Moses pre-existence (i, 14) and the rôle of intercessor in the unseen world (xii, 6). The Midrash contain similar ideas.[1] It is hard however to find evidence for a belief that Moses would appear on earth, like Elijah, to assist in the inauguration of the messianic age. The one known rabbinic saying on the subject is of very uncertain date: 'If I send the prophet Elijah ye must both come together' (Rabbi Johanan ben Zakkai).

Many commentators therefore have seen in the appearance of Moses and Elijah in the Transfiguration story a plain symbol to the disciples of the imminence of the messianic age. Lohmeyer says: 'The entry of Moses and Elijah indicates that the end of time, the day of deliverance and establishment of an everlasting reign of God is imminent.' Boobyer argues more specifically that their appearance provides a picture of the elect accompanying the Messiah at the Parousia.

The reaction of Peter to the sight of the heavenly visitors is to blurt out an apparently stupid remark suggesting that three *tabernacles* should be made. But is the remark stupid? Not so, says Lohmeyer; it represents a right understanding of what is happen-

---

[1] Cf. *Deuteronomy Rabba*, ix, 5: 'In this age thou didst lead my sons, and into the age to come I will lead them by thee.' *Tanchuma B*, vi, 5: 'In this age I made thee to be first, and into the age to come ... thou wilt come first of all.'

THE STUDY OF THE TRANSFIGURATION

ing. It was the hope of Israel that Yahveh would, as of old, tabernacle with His people. Sometimes the hope took the form of a poetic imagery of the tabernacle (Tobit xiii, 10). Sometimes there was a belief that there would be a literal tabernacle in the wilderness once again (Josephus *Ant.* xx, 167, 188; *Bell. Jud.* ii, 259). Sometimes the Feast of Tabernacles was held to have an eschatological reference (Zech. xiv, 16-19). And plainly the words σκηνή and κατασκηνοῦν in the Septuagint blend together the general conception of God tabernacling in Israel and the particular conception of the visible tabernacle. Peter in large measure understands. 'The day of fulfilment is near. Moses and Elijah have appeared. The Lord is here. Let us build "tabernacles" in which you can "tabernacle" for ever.'[1]

How correct was Peter's response! Yet, as Saint Mark records, 'he knew not what he was saying'. And this sentence serves to remind us that though the story of the Transfiguration is filled with current messianic and eschatological ideas it is not simply the creation of these ideas, for it contains a novel element, drawn from the gospel of Jesus, which disturbs these ideas and re-creates them.

[1] Lohmeyer: *Das Evangelium Markus*, p. 176.

CHAPTER XI

THE TRANSFIGURATION IN SAINT MARK

I

THE COMPARISON of the three narratives of the Transfiguration is a fascinating study. *Saint Mark's* account is the earliest and its naïve and primitive features are at once apparent. The quaint description of the intense whiteness of the garments of Jesus; the address 'Rabbi' used by Peter; the acknowledgment of the ignorance implied in Peter's interjection—these are in keeping with those characteristics of Saint Mark's Gospel which many students still regard as signs of its primitive perspective. *Saint Matthew* edits Saint Mark in the interests of the greater theological clarity which he desires: Jesus is likened to Moses on the mount, His face shining; both the parallelism with the scene in Exodus and the Christological motifs are made more explicit. *Saint Luke's* narrative introduces rather wider divergencies, and it is still an unsolved problem how far his deviations from Saint Mark are due to separate sources or to free editorial writing. Here he introduces into the story two elements which have had a vast influence upon its interpretation. It was during the *prayer* of Jesus that the change took place; and the conversation of Moses and Elijah explicitly connects the Transfiguration with the *passion*.

Did the event occur by day or by night? Saint Luke alone suggests the night, by saying that the disciples were 'weighed down with sleep' and saw the glory 'when they awoke'.[1] Perhaps however Saint Luke's language is borrowed from the story of Gethsemane. But indirect evidence for the night time is suggested by the nature of the geography: it is rather unlikely that the ascent of the high mountain, the Transfiguration and the

[1] Perhaps the word διαγρηγορήσαντες means 'keeping awake' (durch-wachen), as Trench and Plummer suggest.

THE TRANSFIGURATION IN SAINT MARK

descent all occurred within a single day. The question remains undecided, but with at least a possibility that the truth is represented in the lines of Armitage Robinson's hymn:

> 'Tis good Lord, to be here:
> Thy glory fills the night.

Now for Saint Mark's narrative:

> And after six days Jesus taketh with him Peter, and James, and John and bringeth them into a high mountain apart by themselves: and he was transfigured before them: And his garments became glistering, exceeding white; so as no fuller on earth can whiten them. And there appeared unto them Elijah with Moses: and they were talking with Jesus. And Peter answereth and saith to Jesus, Rabbi, it is good for us to be here: and let us make three tabernacles; one for thee, and one for Moses, and one for Elijah. For he wist not what to answer; for they became sore afraid. And there came a cloud overshadowing them: and there came a voice out of the cloud, This is my beloved Son: hear ye him. And suddenly looking round about, they saw no one any more, save Jesus only with themselves.

After six days. Nowhere else, outside the story of Holy Week, does Saint Mark note an interval of time. Some have seen in the mention of the six days a piece of symbolism: Moses was six days in the cloud on Mount Sinai before his converse with Yahveh; a priest in the temple purged himself for six days before a feast (Lohmeyer). Others have seen a genuine historical reminiscence. More likely is the view that the note of time marks the connection between two decisive phases in the story (Schlatter).

... a high mountain apart by themselves. Tradition (e.g. Cyril of Jerusalem, *Catech.* xii, 16) has named the site as Tabor. But the presence of a fortress on the summit (cf. Josephus, *Bell. Jud.* iv, 1, 8) tells against this; and there is more likelihood in one of the three spurs of Hermon which rise to about 9,000 feet and overlook Caesarea Philippi. The peaks are free from snow in the summer. The climb is an exhausting one, taking six hours from the nearest point below; and the traveller is 'before long painfully affected by the rarity of the atmosphere'.[1] Here indeed was solitude, with a view which might extend from the sea to

---

[1] See Tristram: *The Land of Israel*, pp. 609–613.

Damascus, from the Lebanon to the mountains of Moab, down the Jordan valley to the Dead Sea, or over Galilee to Jerusalem and beyond it.

... and he was transfigured before them: and his garments became exceeding white; so as no fuller on earth could whiten them. The word μετεμορφώθη tells of a profound change of form (in contrast with mere appearance), without describing its character. Elsewhere it is used of the profound change in the being of a Christian (Rom. xii, 2; 2 Cor. iii, 18). But in amplifying it Saint Mark adds only a reference to the incomparable whiteness of the garments (Codex Bezae: ὡς χιών, like snow).

And there appeared unto them Elijah with Moses: and they were talking with them. The order is peculiar to Saint Mark, and it may be dictated by the greater prominence of Elijah in his gospel. We have examined the background of Jewish ideas and expectations. 'Their appearing shews that the Kingdom of God stands directly at the gate.' (Klostermann, ad. loc.) But have they no personal significance, drawn from their own history and their relation to Jesus with whom they converse? Here the probabilities carry us beyond the limits of the current traditions. (1) They stand for Law and Prophecy: in them Law and Prophecy bear their witness to the Messiah. (2) Yet their significance in the Old Testament cannot be circumscribed within the terms Law and Prophecy. Moses is more than the lawgiver; for he is also prophet prefiguring Him to whom the people will hearken (Deut. xviii, 15), and he is one whose converse with God was mouth to mouth (Num. xii, 8) and face to face (Deut. xxxiv, 10). Elijah is more than the prophet: he is the final precursor of the Messiah, with a unique mission of restoration. Thus by appearing together Moses and Elijah sum up the entire drama of the old order from its beginning to its end: the one is the predecessor, the other is the precursor of the Messiah.[1] (3) But 'mere representativeness is not enough', as Miss Maisie Spens has said. Moses and Elijah were men alive unto God; they had conversed with Him on a mountain; they had served Him and suffered for Him in history, and they had not ceased to be His servants. So now 'they come not as dumb

---

[1] I owe this illuminating suggestion to J. Jeremias's article in *Theologisches Wörterbuch*, II, 930-43. He describes Moses as 'der Vorgänger', and Elijah as 'der Vorläufer'.

apparitions, but are with Jesus in living intercourse and speak with Him: their presence shews His communion with the heavenly world' (Schlatter).

And Peter answereth and saith to Jesus, Rabbi it is good for us to be here: and let us make three tabernacles; one for thee, and one for Moses, and one for Elijah. For he wist not what to answer; for they became sore afraid. Peter's words, καλόν ἐστιν ἡμᾶς ὧδε εἶναι, as translated in R.V., suggest simply the longing to remain in the heavenly scene far from the turmoil of the world below. But a more probable translation is: 'It is a good thing that we are here,' and the words thus lead on to the reason—that we may make three booths. Peter's longing to perpetuate the scene, with the glorious figures housed upon the mount, is blended in his mind with the Feast of Tabernacles and with the imagery of the tabernacling of God with His people. Here and now let the tabernacling begin, with the Messiah and Moses and Elijah dwelling in glory.

Peter was wrong. He erred—because the tabernacling of God with mankind did not depend upon the execution of his suggestion, but upon the fact of the presence of Jesus. Simply by His mission on earth they had the tabernacling presence in their midst.

And there came a cloud overshadowing them. Saint Luke infers that the cloud enveloped all, including the disciples who 'feared as they entered into the cloud'. Saint Mark leaves the point obscure.[1] The νεφέλη ἐπισκιάζουσα is the sign of the presence of the glory; and the promise is being fulfilled that in the messianic age 'the glory of the Lord shall be seen and the cloud' (2 Macc. ii, 7). Jesus, Moses, Elijah are hidden from sight; and the disciples know themselves to be in the presence of God Himself.

... and there came a voice out of the cloud, This is my beloved Son: hear ye him. It is the voice of God who speaks. As at the baptism in Jordan, the voice hails Jesus as 'my Son, the only one': there the words were spoken to Jesus, here to the disciples. They must 'hear him', the prophet to whom the people shall 'hearken' (Deut. xviii, 15, 18). They will find the answer to their quest

[1] Mark's αὐτοῖς does not necessarily include the disciples. Some MSS. read αὐτῷ.

of the age-to-come not in a prolonging of the scene upon the mountain, but in their obedient listening to the word of Jesus. Lohmeyer's commentary strikingly draws out the centrality of the hearing of Jesus as Son of God. 'He is not delivering, sanctifying and glorifying the nation; but He is teaching three disciples who hearken to His word. If Mark elsewhere speaks of the healing and exorcising and does not give prominence to the preaching, here speaking and speech are the only method and the only efficacy of this Son of Man. A Johannine touch rests upon this narrative. That which in John runs through the story of Jesus from beginning to end: $\mu o \nu o \gamma \epsilon \nu \grave{\eta} s \; \Theta \epsilon \grave{o} s \ldots \; \grave{\epsilon} \kappa \epsilon \hat{\imath} \nu o s \; \grave{\epsilon} \xi \eta \gamma \acute{\eta} \sigma a \tau o$ (i, 18, cf. vi, 68) is here shewn once for all in the event (of the Transfiguration) and in the command: $\grave{a} \kappa o \acute{\upsilon} \epsilon \tau \epsilon \; a \grave{\upsilon} \tau o \hat{\upsilon}$."

And what is it to which they must hearken? Before the Transfiguration and again after it He teaches the disciples that the Son of Man must die. He who stood in glory with Moses and Elijah on either side will be crucified with evildoers on the right and on the left; and the three disciples, who heard the Father's voice hail Him as Son, will hear His voice in Gethsemane telling of His obedience to the Father's will. 'They must learn the greatness of his offering—how deep is his fellowship with the Father, and how great is the pain of his soul.' (Schlatter.) *And suddenly looking round about they saw no one any more, save Jesus only with themselves.*

2

The revelation given on the mountain is, even as the earliest Gospel alone describes it, rich in its reference to the past, the present and the future. The old covenant is declared to be summed up and superseded by the Messiah. Jesus is seen in converse with the saints in heaven. The relation of His mission and person to the purpose of God is made known, and the authority of His words as the revelation of the Father receives ratification from on high. Implicit in Saint Mark's narrative are the special themes of the other two Synoptic narratives: in Saint Matthew, the comparison and contrast between Christ and Moses; in Saint Luke, the connection between the Transfiguration and the Cross.

But what is the specific connection between the Transfiguration and the glory? The theme of the latter part of Saint Mark's

THE TRANSFIGURATION IN SAINT MARK

gospel is that first the Son of Man must die and afterwards the Son of Man will come in glory. Plainly therefore the Transfiguration prefigures a glory that lies in the future. But what event precisely does it prefigure?

1. Many scholars have held that the forward reference is to the Resurrection appearances. In the ancient Church this was a frequent interpretation, and modern writers have not been lacking to uphold it.[1] The word δόξα is, as we have seen, used in a number of passages in the New Testament to describe the Resurrection state. It is asked: 'if the disciples were to recognize Jesus when He appeared to them, risen from the dead, would it not be appropriate that Jesus should prepare some of them by a foreshewing of the glory in which He would appear? And does not the command of Jesus to the three disciples to keep the Transfiguration secret until after the Resurrection (Mark ix, 9-10) support this view?'

This last point is criticized by Boobyer. 'My impression is that verses ix, 9, 10 in referring to the Resurrection introduce a *new* topic not associated with the foregoing event.... And what of ix, 9? If at the Transfiguration the disciples were granted a confirmation of the hope of the Resurrection, it was given presumably to sustain the faith of the disciples in the eventual triumph of Jesus over death: it was to be their strength in the dark hours ahead during and immediately after the Passion. Why then the injunction to be silent about it until after the Resurrection? Why was so welcome an aid to faith to be denied to others?' The criticism is not wholly valid, for it does not meet the possibility described long ago by the author of *Pastor Pastorum* that the Transfiguration was designed not to lead the disciples to expect the Resurrection and believe in it before it happened, but to enable some of them, when it had happened, to connect it with the earlier episode and to accept it in that light. Be this as it may, there remains an overwhelming objection to the theory which we are discussing, and Boobyer states it convincingly. There is so little resemblance between the details of the Transfiguration

---

[1] E.g. E. Meyer: *Ursprung und Anfänge des Christentums*, pp. 154 ff; Harnack: *Sitzungsberichte der Preussichen Akademie der Wissenschaften*, 1922, pp. 62-80; H. A. A. Kennedy: *Journal of Theological Studies*, IV, pp. 270-3; Latham: *Pastor Pastorum*, pp. 341-8.

and the circumstances of the Resurrection appearances that it is hard to see how any of the evangelists can have thought of the former as a preparation for the latter. If the transfigured Christ is akin to the descriptions in the Epistles of the glorified state of Christ and the Christians, there is no real correspondence with the descriptions of His appearances to the apostles and the women. It is inconceivable that the evangelists narrated the Transfiguration in the belief that it was a training of the disciples for the appearances of Jesus after His Resurrection.

2. What is the alternative? It is that the Transfiguration foreshadows the Parousia. Here again it is Boobyer who has made the fullest collection of the evidence. Some of his points are unconvincing, as when he connects the 'voice' with the 'shout' with which the Lord will descend at His second coming (1 Thess. iv, 16), or as when he suggests a link between the 'tabernacles' and an alleged Christian use of σκηνή in an eschatological setting (2 Cor. v, 1–4; Luke xvi, 9; Rev. xxi, 1–3). Nor is it certain that the connection of the cloud with the Parousia is more natural than its connection with the presence of the glory on earth as in Exodus.[1] But all the imagery *can* be, and the imagery of light and shining garments is most readily, associated with an eschatological picture of the coming of the Son of Man; and in Saint Mark's Gospel the glory beyond the Passion is emphatically the glory of that coming. The last point seems to be decisive. Peter and his companions on the mountain are spectators in advance of the glory that is going to be declared; and, in Kittel's words, 'seine Verklärung ist Vorwegnahme seiner Eschatologie', His Transfiguration is the anticipation of His eschatology. True, the glory would be Christ's from the hour of His exaltation: it was, as we have seen, the teaching of the primitive Church that Christ was raised up into glory. But, though the glory would be His from the third day, it would become visible to the Church only at His return. This was the glory to which the Transfigura-

---

[1] Each of these points of Boobyer's argument is criticized by Riesenfeld, op. cit., pp. 292–7. He finds some of Boobyer's references to σκηνή 'un peu inconséquent', and he urges that the word ἀκωούω is so often connected with the teaching of Jesus in His earthly ministry that it is unreasonable to connect it with the voice at the Parousia. He also reminds us of the place of the idea of the *post-Resurrection* δόξα of Jesus in the N.T. teaching.

tion points; and the theology of the event, as Saint Mark understands it, is aptly described in the words of Saint Anselm: 'suam suorumque glorificationem praemonstravit'.

Such is the interpretation which lies most plain upon the surface of the Marcan gospel. But the significance of the event is not wholly futurist, and Boobyer seems to fall into a false simplification when he so treats it. The Transfiguration does indicate that the messianic age is already being realized: Jesus *is* the Messiah, the Kingdom of God *is* here, the age to come *is* breaking into this world. If the message of the Transfiguration is one with our Lord's predictions of the Parousia it is also one with His sayings concerning present fulfilment: 'Blessed are the eyes which see the things which ye see: for I say unto you that many kings and prophets desired to see the things which ye see and have not seen them; and to hear the things which ye hear and have not heard them' (Luke x, 23-4). In view of Mark's emphasis upon the note of realization in the words and deeds of Jesus he cannot be unmindful of this when he records the Transfiguration. The glory is the glory already present because the Messiah is here.

Though Mark does not dwell upon the pre-existence of Christ, his gospel is the gospel of the Son of God. Beside the contrast between the future events of the Passion and the Parousia there is the ever-present contrast between the Divine Sonship and the earthly ministry wherein the Divine Son is hidden and humiliated. On the mount of Transfiguration a veil is withdrawn, and the glory which the disciples are allowed to see is not only the glory of a future event, but the glory of Him who *is* the Son of God.

CHAPTER XII

THE TRANSFIGURATION IN OTHER NEW TESTAMENT WRITERS

THE TRANSFIGURATION is an event to which the words might specially be applied; 'What I do thou knowest not now, but thou shalt understand hereafter.' The story is interpreted in the later narratives of Saint Matthew and Saint Luke, and its influence is reflected in the theology of the Fourth Evangelist with traces in other parts of the New Testament. These interpretations now call for our study, and in the case of one of the interpreters—Saint Luke—we may find that he offers not only his own theologizing but also some fresh historical information about what happened.

Saint Matthew

The Matthaean story is so close to the Marcan that little needs to be said of it. But the editorial alterations are significant:

> And he was transfigured before them: and *his face did shine as the sun*, and his garments became white *as the light*. . . . Behold a *bright* cloud ($\phi\omega\tau\epsilon\iota\nu\acute{\eta}$) overshadowed them (Matt. xvii, 2, 5).

The resemblance to the scene on Mount Sinai is made plain. Moses went up into the Mount, and after six days in the cloud he saw the glory of the LORD; and when he came down to the people the skin of his face shone. Here in contrast is the new and greater Moses, whose face shines not with a reflected glory but with the unborrowed glory as of the sun's own rays. Thus is the old covenant utterly surpassed by the new, 'for if that which passeth away was with glory, how much more that which remaineth is in glory' (2 Cor. iii, 11).

As at Sinai, it is the voice that makes them afraid.

> And when the disciples heard it, they fell on their face and were sore afraid. And Jesus came and touched them and said, Arise, and be not afraid (Matt. xvii, 6–7).

IN OTHER NEW TESTAMENT WRITERS

The scene quivers with an awe like the awe of Sinai. Only Jesus can free them from their fear, and He comes and bids them to fear not.

Saint Luke

In Saint Luke's account the reader is less conscious of the terrors of Sinai than of the serenity of the Son of Man wrapt in communion with the Father.

> And *it came to pass about eight days* after *these sayings,* he took with him Peter and John and James, and *went* up into the mountain *to pray.* And *as he was praying the fashion of his countenance was altered,* and his *raiment* became *white and dazzling.* And behold, there talked with him *two* men, which were Moses and Elijah; *who appeared in glory: and spake of his decease which he was about to accomplish at Jerusalem. Now Peter and they that were with him were heavy with sleep: but when they were fully awake they saw his glory: and the two men that stood with him. And it came to pass: as they were parting from him,* Peter said unto Jesus, *Master,* it is good for us to be here: and let us make three tabernacles; one for thee, and one for Moses and one for Elijah: not knowing what *he said.* And while he said these things there came a cloud, and overshadowed them: and they feared *as they entered into the cloud.* And a voice came out of the cloud, saying, This is my son, *the chosen:* hear ye him. And when *the voice came,* Jesus was found alone. And *they held their peace,* and told no man *in those days* any of those things which they had seen (Luke ix, 28–36).

The words in italics indicate how considerable are the divergencies from Saint Mark's narrative; but, though some scholars have postulated that Saint Luke is drawing upon another source, the more probable explanation is that he is rewriting his Marcan source freely. In so doing he introduces two special motifs: the connection between the Transfiguration and the prayer of Jesus, the recognition by Moses and Elijah of the relation between the Transfiguration and the Cross.

1. Omitting the word 'transfigured' lest it should suggest a pagan sort of metamorphosis Saint Luke relates that Jesus sought 'the mountain' to pray, and that 'in his prayer' (ἐν τῷ προσεύχεσθαι) his face and his raiment became filled with dazzling light. 'The mountain' suggests a hill in Galilee whither Jesus is wont to withdraw. Saint Luke is careless of topography, and he has not

GLORY AND TRANSFIGURATION

recorded that Caesarea Philippi was the scene of Peter's confession.

Saint Luke is relating the event to the inner life of Jesus. To a greater extent than any other evangelist he is a biographer, concerned to trace not only the proclaiming by Jesus of a divine gospel but the growth of the manhood of Jesus and the inner conflicts through which it passed to the perfecting of its destiny in the Passion and the Resurrection. 'Jesus advanced in wisdom and stature, and in favour with God and man.' 'I have a baptism to be batized with, and how am I straitened until it be accomplished.' Beneath the outward happenings of the ministry there were the unceasing spiritual trials, and in these Jesus was glad that the disciples could in some measure share (Luke xxii, 28). It is from this point of view that Saint Luke describes the Transfiguration. It is an inner crisis in the life of Jesus. The vocation of the Cross has been accepted; Jesus is communing with the Father, and His submission to the Father's will that He must suffer has its counterpart in the shining around Him of the radiance of the glory of God. As for the disciples, they are more than spectators, for perhaps, by describing *their* entry into the cloud and the accompanying fear which they experience, Saint Luke is picturing them as plunging after their Master into the new and dread stage of their calling.

May it not be that Saint Luke's description, despite its secondary and editorial character, takes us near to the history of what really happened? His frequent references in his Gospel to the praying of Jesus are of course editorial additions (Luke iii, 21; vi, 12; ix, 18; ix, 28; xi, 1). Yet they may be drawn from a genuine knowledge of a factor in the traditions about Jesus; for the story of Jesus praying in a desert place a great while before day in Mark i, 35-9 seems to be a *typical* episode. Hence it is possible that Saint Luke in his Transfiguration narrative, while writing as a theological interpreter, is in fact giving us good history. It is hardly fanciful to think of Jesus, alone with three disciples not long after the first prediction of the Passion, undergoing a conflict of pain and self-committal; and as He bends His will in obedience the glory is made visible.

2. Saint Luke's other special motif is the linking of the glory and the Passion. He tells his readers that Moses and Elijah were

IN OTHER NEW TESTAMENT WRITERS

speaking of 'his *exodus* which he was about to accomplish at Jerusalem'.

The word ἔξοδος can mean departure from the world in death, and that meaning is suggested here by the contrast with the word εἴσοδος used in Acts xiii, 24 of the coming of Christ into the world. The Rheims version of 1582 has 'decease', the version of Tyndale has 'departure'. But what a wealth of meaning the departure of Christ at Jerusalem contains! 'Verbum valde grave', says Bengel, 'in quo continetur Passio, Crux, Mors, Resurrectio, Ascensio'; and there is also, in Christ's departure, the new exodus of Israel from bondage into freedom. Of this Moses and Elijah were speaking from the midst of the glory.

In both of his special motifs in the story of the Transfiguration Saint Luke is not far from the doctrines of Saint John. The 'while he was praying' is not far from the glorifying of the Father by the Son; and the exodus in Jerusalem is not far from the words: 'I came out from the Father, and am come into the world; again I leave the world, and go unto the Father' (John xvi, 28).

The Fourth Gospel

Saint John does not record the Transfiguration: the glory which in the Synoptics flashes into the story on the mountain is perceived by Saint John to pervade all the words and works of Jesus. Loisy wrote with justice:

> Le quatrième Evangile est une théophanie perpetuelle où la scene de transfiguration qui est décrite dans les Synoptiques ne pouvait être maintenue n'y ayant plus de raison d'être et se trouvait, comme conception, bien au dessous de la gloire qui éclate dans tous les discours et dans tous les actes du Verbe incarné.[1]

The disappearance of the Transfiguration story in the Fourth Gospel has a parallel in the disappearance of the agony in Gethsemane. But in neither case does the disappearance imply that the evangelist is unmindful of the importance of the event. Far from it: for, as Hoskyns pointed out, by omitting these two incidents he leads his readers to realize that the truth represented by them belongs not to the incidents in isolation but to the life

---
[1] *Le Quatrième Evangile*, p. 105.

of Jesus as a whole. It is not only in the garden of Gethsemane that Jesus bends His will in utter submission to the Father's will for the salvation of mankind; and it is not only on Mount Hermon that the glory of Jesus is manifested as He sets His face towards death. Rather 'the heavenly glory of Jesus and His troubled humiliation are shewn to condition every part of His life';[1] and in the episode where He prays: 'save me from this hour' and the voice from heaven is heard (John xii, 27–8) these two elements in the Christology are set forth together. Again, it is not only on Mount Hermon that the witness of law and prophecy to the Son of God is displayed, for 'the story of the Fourth Gospel sets the glory of the only Son on a mount of Transfiguration with Moses and the new Elijah (the greatest of the prophets) on either hand to bear witness to that glory'.[2] The relation of the Fourth Gospel to the earlier traditions of the ministry of Jesus involves some unsolved problems, but there are reasons for suspecting that the Transfiguration—like the Baptism of Jesus and the Institution of the Eucharist—was omitted not because John did not know of it but because he understood its meaning so well.

The Second Epistle of Saint Peter

The reference to the Transfiguration in this Epistle has an importance which the pseudonymous character of the work has caused to be somewhat overlooked. It tells us much of the interpretation of the Transfiguration in the early Church.

It is certain that this work is not by Saint Peter, but by a second-century writer who uses Saint Peter's name for the purpose of combating false and un-apostolic teaching. 'The author of Second Peter', says Moffatt, 'has First Peter before him, as well as the tract of Judas; but he writes with much less ease and lucidity. His object is to controvert the dangerous teachers of his age, and he does so by appealing to the prestige of Saint Peter as the representative of the primitive, orthodox faith. The literary device was recognized in those days. It was a development of the method which allowed an historian to compose speeches for characters in his narrative, and an author evidently felt no

[1] E. C. Hoskyns: *The Fourth Gospel*, Vol. I, p. 86.
[2] L. S. Thornton: *The Common Life in the Body of Christ*, p. 413.

IN OTHER NEW TESTAMENT WRITERS

scruple about adopting this literary device in order to win a hearing for counsels which he felt to be both timely and inspired.'[1]

The first chapter of the book, florid though the style is, has singular beauty. 'Peter' exhorts his readers so to live that they may make their calling sure and be ready for the glory prepared for them in Christ's eternal kingdom. He for his part will continue, so long as he lives, to remind them of these things; and after his death he will leave behind him something that will serve to remind them still (perhaps this is a reference to Saint Mark's Gospel). Then he continues:

> For we did not follow cunningly devised fables, when we made known unto you the power and coming (παρουσία) of our Lord Jesus Christ, but we were eye-witnesses of his majesty. For he received from God the Father honour and glory, when there came such a voice from the excellent glory, This is my beloved Son, in whom I am well pleased: and this voice we ourselves heard come out of heaven, when we were with him in the holy mount. And we have the word of prophecy made more sure; whereunto ye do well to take heed, as unto a lamp shining in a dark place, until the day dawn and the day star arise in your hearts: knowing this first, that no prophecy of scripture is of private interpretation. For no prophecy ever came by the will of man: but men spake from God, being moved by the Holy Ghost (2 Pet. i, 16–21).

Here the Transfiguration is described, with phrases from Saint Matthew and Saint Luke. But language more elaborate and more honorific is also used. The word for 'eye-witneses', ἐππόται, was used of the initiates of the Eleusinian mysteries. The word for 'majesty', μεγαλειότης, is very rare in the New Testament; and the phrase 'the excellent glory', ἡ μεγαλοπρεπής δόξα, is a reverential paraphrase for God (cf. Test. Levi 3; Enoch xiv, 18, 20; cii, 3). 'Peter's' claim to be a witness of the Transfiguration is his lofty credential for the teaching which he is addressing to his readers.

But why has the Transfiguration this high importance, being cited even in preference to the Resurrection? (1) It was a proof of the coming Parousia of Jesus Christ. Those who witnessed it

---
[1] *The General Epistles*, Moffatt commentary, p. 174.

saw in anticipation 'the power and coming of Jesus Christ'. (2) It bore witness to the prophetic word. It confirmed the truth of the whole body of prophetic teaching which spoke of the messianic age. This for 'Peter' is the supreme importance of the Transfiguration: 'we have the word of prophecy made more sure' (Moffatt, 'we have gained fresh confirmation of the prophetic word'). It shews that the prophets are not annulled. Vindicated and confirmed by the Transfiguration, their word endures into the Christian era. It is like a lamp in a dark place, bringing the illumination of the Gospel until the light of the Parousia shines within the hearts of Christ's people.

'Peter' is making a point of great importance. If the narratives of the Transfiguration in the Gospels shew that the Old Testament bears witness to Jesus the Messiah, 'Peter' is concerned to shew the converse truth: that the Transfiguration bears witness to the permanent validity of the Old Testament. It is a distortion of the truth to say (like Marcion, and many moderns) that the Transfiguration shews the supersession of the Old Testament by the Gospel, for 'the fulfilment of the Old Testament' means not its abolition but its vindication as a perpetual witness to the supremacy of Christ.

Some Other Writers

Such are the clear illustrations of the impact of the story of the Transfiguration upon the thought of the Christians of the first century and beyond. Elsewhere there are passages which shew, if not evidence of the influence of the Transfiguration, at least a congruity between the traditions of the event and the thought of the Church.

One instance is the description in the Epistle to the Hebrews of Christ 'crowned with glory and honour, that by the grace of God he should taste death for every man' (Heb. ii, 9). The picture of Christ glorified before His Passion and seeking death as one already invested with glory is utterly congruous with the story of the Transfiguration. More than this it is impossible to regard as certain. Yet the further possibility cannot be excluded that the writer, who cherishes greatly the traditions of the earthly life of Jesus and dwells especially upon the episode of

IN OTHER NEW TESTAMENT WRITERS

Gethsemane (in v, 7-8), may have the event of the Transfiguration specifically in mind.

Nor can the possibility be ignored that when Christians coveted eagerly the sight of Jesus at the Parousia their idea of the vision of Him was fed by the Transfiguration-story. A striking instance of this possibility (1 Pet. v, 1) has been mentioned already (p. 42). At the revelation of Jesus Christ 'whom not having seen ye love' (1 Pet. i, 8) they would see Him not as He was in the days of His earthly ministry but 'as He is' (1 John iii, 2); and a glimpse of Jesus 'as He is' was afforded only by the memory of what three disciples saw upon the holy mount. So hard is that vision that it will be recaptured only by those who are 'transformed into his image' (2 Cor. iii, 18) or 'made like him' (1 John iii, 2). The vision of Christ is the transfiguration of man.

CHAPTER XIII

THE TRANSFIGURATION IN THE CHURCH

I—The Transfiguration in Christian Festivals

THE FOURTEENTH-CENTURY historian Nicephorus Callixtus says that in about the year A.D. 326 the Empress Helena had a church built upon Mount Tabor, endowed it generously and made it easily accessible to pilgrims by a staircase of marble on the mountain-side. It would be rash to be confident of this very late evidence either for the event or for the date. But the excavations made in Mount Tabor by the Franciscans have disclosed the existence of two churches there, one built by the crusaders and the other dating probably from the fourth or fifth century.[1] Tabor was the seat of a bishop present at the fifth council of Constantinople in 553. The commemoration of the holy Transfiguration (ἡ Ἁγια Μεταμόρφωσις) was widespread throughout the East. It appears on August 6th in the Byzantine and Ethiopic kalendars, and on the seventh Sunday after Pentecost in the Armenian. If the 'Menology of Constantinople' be the work of John of Damascus the observance can be ascribed to the eighth century. Such is the appeal of the Transfiguration to the Eastern mind that its commemoration takes a place in the Eastern Orthodox Church of equal rank with Christmas, Epiphany, Ascension and Pentecost, yielding in importance only to Easter (ἡ Ἑορτή). A solemn day called a 'proheortia' precedes August 6th, and an octave or 'apodosis' follows it.

In the West the recognition of the Transfiguration was slower, and it has never reached the height attained in the East. As early as the fifth century the Transfiguration was commemorated on the Ember Saturday in Lent and on the Sunday following. The Gospel for these days in the Roman rite is Saint Matthew's narrative of the Transfiguration, and there is no reason to

[1] M. de Vogüe: Le Mont Tabor, Paris 1900.

THE TRANSFIGURATION IN THE CHURCH

doubt that the rule is at least as old as the time of Pope Leo's famous sermon on the Transfiguration. But there are also traces of a commemoration on August 6th. A Spanish bishop, Eldeforst, in 845, refers to it.[1] An MS. of the eleventh century[2] in the Vatican has a note for August 6th in the kalendar: 'Transformavit St. Dominus in monte coram apostolis tribus, Moysen scilicet Eleiaque gloria perstitit medius, Xisti. Bened. uvae. Felicissimi et Agapiti.' In 1152 a priest of Prum named Potho, in complaining of the multiplication of Feasts through the influence of the monastic orders, mentions the Transfiguration as one of the novelties which he laments; and it seems that in the same century the Abbey of Cluny had adopted and propagated the commemoration.[3] But the decisive step was taken only in 1457 when Pope Callixtus ordered the general observance of August 6th as the Feast of the Transfiguration, desiring by so doing to commemorate the victory of the Hungarians over the Turks at Belgrade. Henceforth the Festival was universal, and known as *Festum Transfigurationis Domini*. The Epistle is 2 Peter i, 16-19, the gospel is Matthew xvii, 1-9. The Roman Collect runs:

> Deus, qui fidei sacramenta in Unigeniti tui gloriosa Transfiguratione patrum testimonia roborasti et adoptionem filiorum perfectam voce delapsa in nube lucida mirabiliter praesignasti; concede propitius ut ipsius Regis gloriae nos cohaeredes efficias, et ejusdem gloriae tribuas esse consortes....

The Sarum collect has a somewhat different emphasis:

> Deus, qui hodierna die tuum mirabiliter transfigurationem coelitus utriusque testamenti patribus revelasti; da nobis, quaesumus, beneplacitis tibi actibus, ad ejus semper contemplandam pertingere gloriam; in quo paternitati optime complacuisse tentatus es.

In the rites of East and West alike there is included on this day a prayer for the blessing of the grapes:

[1] Quoted in Thomassin: *Traités Historiques et Dogmatiques*, tom ii, 1683.
[2] Quoted in Ebner: *Quellen und Forschungen*.
[3] Batiffol: *Histoire du Bréviaire Romain*, p. 163.

GLORY AND TRANSFIGURATION

II—*The Transfiguration in the Fathers*

Commemorated both in East and West the Transfiguration inevitably had its place in the patristic homilies and expositions of the scriptures. And many of the recurring themes of exegesis are common to East and West.

Sometimes much allegory is used. Thus Origen, in the course of a long treatment of the Transfiguration in his Commentary on Saint Matthew, equates the garments of Jesus with the sayings of the scriptures, which are mere words to the natural man but white and luminous to those who have made the ascent of discipleship. 'Fullers on earth may be considered to be the wise of this world, who are thought to adorn even their foul understandings and doctrines with a false whiteness drawn from their own minds.' And Augustine identifies the raiment with the Church, participating as she does in the radiant holiness of the Lord (*Sermon* LXXVIII).

Such elaborate allegorizing is however less prominent in most of the Fathers than the exposition of the more direct implications of the Transfiguration story. A constantly recurring theme is the *unity of the scriptures*. Tertullian deals with this matter in a long and brilliant passage of debate with Marcion. Marcion had claimed to find in the Transfiguration an argument for his thesis that the God of the New Testament was in conflict with the Creator God of the Old: for on the mount Christ was honoured, and Moses and Elijah were dishonoured beside Him. Tertullian asks: 'Ought you not to be ashamed for permitting Him to appear on the mountain in the company of Moses and Elias whom He had come to destroy? . . . This is how he shews them to be aliens, by keeping their own company! This is how he destroys them: he irradiates them with his own glory!' So far from suggesting a conflict between the creator God and the redeemer God the event shews the creator's own cloud and light and heaven and air serving the glory of Christ. Putting the presence of Moses on Sinai side by side with his presence on Tabor Tertullian concludes: 'And with his glory (Moses) went away enlightened from Christ, just as he did of old from the Creator; as *then* to dazzle the eyes of the children of Israel so *now* to smite those of the blinded Marcion, who has failed to see how this

THE TRANSFIGURATION IN THE CHURCH

argument also turns against him' (*Adversus Marcionem* iv, 22). Elsewhere we find the point made in a terser and less controversial way. So Origen: 'By this it is shewn that the glory of the Law and the Prophets had then been displayed, when Christ had been transfigured in glory, so that illumined by His glory Law and Prophecy, with the veil of the letter removed, may be understood in the Spirit' (*Commentary on Romans*, ii, 5). So Jerome: 'Thou dost err, Peter; and, as another evangelist says, knowest not what thou sayest. Think not to seek three tabernacles, when there is *one* tabernacle of the gospel in which law and prophets are to be recapitulated. But if thou seekest three tabernacles do not make the servants equal with the Lord, but make three tabernacles: one for the Father, one for the Son, one for the Holy Ghost: that they whose Divinity is one may have but one tabernacle—in thy bosom' (*In Matthew*, ad. loc.). So too Augustine: 'He desired three tabernacles; the heavenly answer showed him that we have One, whom human judgment sought to divide. Christ the word, the word in the law, the word in the prophets. Why, Peter, seekest thou to divide them?' (*Sermon* LXXVIII).

The Transfiguration foreshadows the *future glory* of *Christ and the Christians*. Sometimes this is thought of in connection with the Parousia. Thus Basil describes: 'Peter and the sons of thunder saw His beauty on the mountain, outshining the brightness of the sun, and they were deemed worthy to receive the anticipation of His glorious parousia with their eyes ($\tau\grave{\alpha}$ $\pi\rho οο ίμια$ $\tau\hat{\eta}\varsigma$ $\dot{\epsilon}\nu\delta \acute{o}\xi ου$ $α\dot{υ}\tau ο\hat{υ}$ $\pi αρουσ ίας$)' (*Hom. in Psalm xlv*, 5). And Theodoret explains that Christ 'taught by these signs the manner of His second Epiphany' (*Epistle*, 145). But more often the Fathers connect the Transfiguration with the Resurrection. Origen and Jerome claimed that the narrative illustrated their respective theories of the risen body. Leo the Great says: 'The foundation was laid of the life of the Church, that the whole body of Christ might realize the character of the change which it would receive, and that the members might promise themselves a share in that honour which had already shone forth in their head' (*Sermon* LI). Gregory the Great says tersely: 'In transfiguratione quid aliud quam resurrectionis ultima gloria nuntiatur?' (*Moral.* xxxii, 6.) And centuries later Anselm summed up the belief:

'Non formam humani corporis amisit, sed suam suorumque glorificationem praemonstravit.'

Sometimes the Fathers identify the cloud with the Spirit. So Ambrose explains: 'It is the overshadowing of the divine spirit which does not darken, but reveals secrets to the hearts of men.' Hence the Transfiguration is a *revelation of the Holy Trinity*. Nowhere is this more beautifully expressed than by the Venerable Bede: 'We must observe that as when the Lord was baptized in Jordan, so on the mountain, covered with brightness, the whole mystery of the Holy Trinity is declared, because we see in the resurrection that glory of the Trinity which we confess in baptism and shall praise it all together. Not in vain does the Holy Spirit appear here in the cloud, there in the form of a dove, seeing that he who now preserves with a simple heart the faith which he receives, shall then in the light of open vision look upon those things which he believed' (*Homily, xxviii*).

Sometimes the Fathers see the Transfiguration as the fulfilment of the prediction of our Lord that some of the disciples 'shall in no wise taste of death till they see the kingdom of God come with power' (Mark ix, 1). Matthew had interpreted this as referring to the Parousia (Matt. xvi, 28), but since the Parousia had not occurred in the apostolic age it was natural to seek other explanations. Hence the saying was applied to the Transfiguration. We find this exegesis in the *Excerpts of Theodotus* of Clement of Alexandria where we read: 'He did not do it (viz. the Transfiguration) for his own sake when he shewed himself, but for the sake of the Church ... that it might learn his advancement (προκόπην) after his departure from the flesh ... and it was necessary for the saying to be fulfilled "there are some who shall not taste of death until they see ...", so they saw and fell asleep' (iv, 1–3).[1] Origen criticized this view as 'unspiritual', but it appears in Chrysostom and other writers. Chrysostom bases a grand sermon on the Transfiguration upon this very text (Matt. xvi, 28). In it he deals specially with the character of Saint Peter, linking the scene with other episodes in Peter's life. He gives five reasons for the presence of Moses and Elijah. The first is that the disciples who had heard the multitude say that Jesus was one of

---

[1] The *Excerpts* are Valentinian gnostic in character, but it is possible that Clement interpolated passages of his own, cf. Boobyer, op. cit., p. 28.

the prophets might see the difference between the Son and the servants. The second is that Moses and Elijah, men jealous for the glory of God, might testify that Jesus was no blasphemer in His divine claims. The third is that He might shew that He has power over life and death. The fourth is that Moses and Elijah may console the disciples by speaking of the glory of the Cross (Chrysostom's text of Luke ix, 31 reads δόξαν for ἔξοδον). And the fifth is that the excellence of Moses and Elijah, as men who for God's laws lost their lives in order to find them, may be seen. But though Chrysostom sees in the Transfiguration a fulfilment already of Christ's prediction, he shews admirably its connection with the Resurrection and its *faint* prefiguring of the Second Coming. 'For not thus shall He come hereafter. For whereas then, to spare His disciples, He discovered so much only of His brightness as they were able to bear; hereafter He shall come in the very glory of the Father, not with Moses and Elias only, but with the infinite host of the Angels . . . not having a cloud over His head, but even Heaven itself being folded up.'

But amongst all the patristic literature which refers to the Transfiguration a place of honour perhaps belongs to the *Sermon of Pope Leo* devoted to the event. Preached on the Ember Saturday in Lent upon the gospel for the day, it gathers up nearly every aspect of the theology of the Transfiguration and presents it with a striking lucidity and vigour and with a practical bearing upon the Christian life.

The preacher begins with Peter's confession of faith in Jesus Christ. It was a faith in the glorious godhead of the Son, and it won from Christ the fullness of blessing. But Peter also needed to be instructed on 'the mystery of Christ's lower nature', both as to its true humanity and as to its glory through union with the divine person. This lesson was conveyed by the teaching of the necessity of Christ's death; but, lest this teaching be unbearable, Christ took the three disciples to the mountain and there, transfigured, He shewed them 'the kingly brilliance which belonged to the nature of His assumed manhood'. Hence 'in this Transfiguration the foremost object was to remove the offence of the Cross from the disciples' heart,[1] and to prevent their faith

[1] 'in qua transfiguratione illud quidem principaliter agebatur, ut de cordibus discipulorum crucis scandalum tolleretur.'

being disturbed by the humiliation of His voluntary Passion by revealing to them the excellence of His hidden dignity. But with no less foresight, the foundation was laid of the Church's life, that the whole body of Christ might realize the character of the change which it would have to receive, and that the members might promise themselves a share in that honour which had already shone forth in their Head.' Thus the event both makes the Cross bearable, and prefigures the Resurrection, a prediction illustrated by quotations from Romans viii, 18, and Colossians iii, 3.

Then the presence of Moses and Elijah shews the unity of the two covenants. Christ, once foretold under the veils of typology, is now seen clearly in His glory. And in fulfilling law and prophecy 'He both teaches the truth of prophecy by His presence, and renders the commandments possible by His grace'. This revelation excites Peter to scorn things earthly and to be 'seized with a sort of frenzied craving for the things eternal', and he desires to make his abode with Jesus on the scene of the glory. But the Lord made no response to Peter's request, indicating that 'what he wished was not indeed wicked, but contrary to the divine order', since the world could not be saved except by Christ's death. 'The joyousness of reigning cannot precede the times of suffering.'

Then the bright cloud and the voice revealed both the divine Son and the Father; and the disciples fell upon their faces, 'for now they had a deeper insight into the undivided Deity of both; and in their fear they did not separate the one from the other, because they doubted not in their faith.' The Son is coeternal with the Father. ' "This is my son", who sought not by grasping and seized not in greediness that equality with Me which He has, but, remaining in the form of My glory, . . . He lowered the unchangeable Godhead even to the form of a slave.' 'Hear ye Him . . . by whose humiliation I am glorified . . . whom the mysteries of the law have foretold, whom the mouths of prophets have sung . . . who redeems the world by His blood . . . who opens the way to heaven, and by the punishment of the Cross prepares for you the steps of ascent to the Kingdom. . . . Why tremble ye at being redeemed? Let that happen which Christ wills and I will.' Thus by the holy Gospel be fortified to suffer for Christ: 'since all our weakness was assumed by Him, we conquer as He conquered and receive what He has promised.'

So ends Pope Leo's sermon. He has shewn his hearers see within the Transfiguration the pattern of the Christian faith and of the Christian calling.

III—*The Transfiguration in the East*

The history of the Eastern theology of the Transfiguration confronts us with some of the deeper divergencies between Eastern and Western Christianity. The East has dwelt upon the cosmic effects of the redemption wrought by Christ, and has viewed the Christian life in terms of our participation within the new creation. It is an outlook mystical rather than moral. The West, moral rather than mystical in its emphasis, has dwelt rather upon the justification and sanctification of human lives, sometimes slipping into a moralism or legalism which misses the cosmic context in which the Christian life is set. The East has so regarded the Cross in the light of the Resurrection as sometimes to make it seem to be robbed of its own special significance and be absorbed into the glory of Easter. The West on the other hand has too often isolated the Cross from the Resurrection. It is in keeping with these contrasts that the East has instinctively honoured the Transfiguration and dwelt upon its meaning with a special warmth and tenacity. While some Western expositors have asked what moral and practical lessons are to be learnt from the event, the East has often been content simply to rejoice in the glory which Mount Tabor sheds upon Christ, the Christians and all creation.

There is a curious work from the ancient Armenian Church entitled *The Revelation of the Lord to Saint Peter*. It was translated into English in 1924, but has never become easily accessible to English readers.[1] It is a homily upon the Transfiguration, utterly unlike the sermon of Pope Leo. Lacking the terseness, the orderliness and the note of dogmatic definition in the Latin work it is a rambling meditation upon the Transfiguration from Peter's point of view. Yet for all the quaint fancies which it contains

[1] The translation is by F. C. Conybeare in *Zeitschrift für Neutestamentliche Wissenschaft*, 1924, pp. 8-17.

there is no trace of the fantastic; its doctrine is orthodox and it seems to belong to one of the main streams of oriental Christianity.

Peter is left by our Lord's predictions in the sickness of the fear of death, the disease of worldly-mindedness that cannot rise to an acceptance of Christ's death and to a faith in His victory over it. Then on the mountain there comes the revelation of Christ glorified, bringing near the awfulness of heaven and the assurance that the portals of death are broken. Moses and Elijah by their presence attest the resurrection of the dead. 'There is not in this mountain any reign of death, and to this mountain death fears to ascend.' Could not the salvation of mankind then be wrought without the death of Christ? 'They ventured to ask the Lord, who knew the secrets of their hearts. . . . But our Lord distressed not His beloved servants, but referred the question for answer to His Father's will.' Such was the revelation, hidden from all and sundry but given to the chosen three, 'the luminous mystery to the children of light . . . and with the same light they were illumined and illumined until the second epiphany of that light'. Abruptly the homily passes to a description of Tabor as the writer knows it. It is a beautiful place with wells of water, 'vines yielding wine worthy for a king to drink' and many olive trees on the slopes. A zigzag path leads to the summit, where are now three churches. The pilgrim will find a brotherhood living there, tilling the land, tending the fruit, working at handicrafts, and so dividing their rule that an unceasing service of praise is offered as they 'make glorious and with awestruck voices adorn the holy churches on their mountain. One of the churches they call the Lord's Church, and the others are dedicated to Moses and Elias.' 'Because they resemble angels, they not only shew mutual love, but no one hides from his fellows his secret thoughts.' 'And I, the most afflicted of men who trod on foot in the Lord's track on that mountain and with my eyes beheld that wonderful congregation of brethren, pray my readers and hearers that they may offer prayer for myself and for you in common. With them may ye escape the dread sentence of God and become worthy of the kingdom of heaven.'

In this homily from the Armenian mountains there is a glimpse of some of the constant characteristics of Eastern Chris-

THE TRANSFIGURATION IN THE CHURCH

tianity: the sense of the dominance of the Resurrection, the unity of the Cross and the Resurrection, the vivid realization of the communion of saints, the contemplative life as a life to which the heavens are opened, the insistence that nature is not left behind but is transformed by Christ in the same new creation wherein the souls of men are drawn into union with God. It is not difficult to grasp how it is that the Transfiguration made its appeal to the Eastern Christians: it came to be treated less an event amongst other events and a dogma amongst other dogmas than a symbol of something which pervades all dogma and all worship. Nowhere is the ethos of Eastern orthodoxy far from the themes which the Transfiguration embodies. In the liturgy for instance the sense of the nearness of heaven and earth is vividly realized; and the triumphant note struck at the offertory means that when the Church commemorates the Passion in the canon of the rite it has already exulted in the presence of Christ risen and victorious.

The services for the Feast of the Transfiguration tell their own tale. At Vespers on the eve the words are sung:

> Before thy Crucifixion, O Christ, the Mount became like unto the heavens, and a cloud was outspread like a canopy, while thou wast transfigured, and while the Father bore witness unto thee, there was Peter, together with James and John, inasmuch as they desired to be with thee at the time of thy betrayal also; that, having beheld thy marvels, they might not be affrighted at thy sufferings. Make us also worthy to adore the same in peace, for the sake of thy great mercy.
>
> Before thy Crucifixion, O Lord, having taken thy disciples into a high mountain, thou wast transfigured before them, dazzling them with rays of light; being desirous to show unto them the radiance of the Resurrection; both because of thy love toward mankind and for the sake of thy power. Vouchsafe the same unto us in peace, O God, inasmuch as thou art merciful and lovest mankind.
>
> When the Saviour was transfigured on the high mountain, having with Him the chief disciples, He became most gloriously radiant, showing that inasmuch as He was radiant with the height of virtues, they also would be vouchsafed divine glory. Moses and Elijah, who talked with Christ made manifest that he ruleth both the quick and the dead, and that he is the God who spake of old through the Law and the Prophets. And unto him also did the voice of the Father

from the cloud bear witness, saying: Hear ye Him, who hath taken hell captive by His Cross, and giveth life everlasting unto the dead.

Linking the feast with the Cross, the Resurrection and the communion of saints the services link it also with the primeval light which shone at the creation and with the light of the new creation wherein all things are transformed.

O thou who didst disseminate the primeval radiance of the light, that thy works may sing thee in the light, O Christ their creator: guide thou our paths in the light.

If the Transfiguration is thus prominent in the general tradition of the East, there are also the special conceptions characteristic of later Russian theology. Here the idea of Transfiguration is employed not as in the Greek Fathers in strict association with the event in the Gospel, but as broadly symbolizing the metamorphosis of the world which has been wrought by the Resurrection of Christ. 'It is not man alone', writes Nicholas Arseniev, 'who is affected by the redemption and the joy of victory; with the joy over our resurrection is linked also joy over the redemption of the whole world, over the ending of the dominance of corruption, over the redemption of all creation and the dawn of the kingdom of life. And the eye of the spirit gazes fervently out towards the glory to come—that "splendid freedom of the children of God" of which all creation shall partake. The resurrection is thus an event of cosmic significance, and the world equally with man, is thereby permeated by the radiance of the celestial glory, although as yet in hidden form, and has attained to a new and high worth; for it has already taken unto itself the germ of immortality.'[1] In this context of thought the word 'transfiguration' is used, sometimes with reference to the event wherein these conceptions are signally symbolized, but more often without such reference and with an awareness simply of the fruits of the Resurrection. Here come also the kindred conceptions of *theosis* and *opsis*. *Theosis* is the transformation of the soul into union with deity. *Opsis* is the vision which accompanies this spiritual growth. It may take the form of the perception by faith of the divine transfiguring power at work in the world, or

[1] *Mysticism and the Eastern Church*, p. 35.

THE TRANSFIGURATION IN THE CHURCH

it may take the form of actual visions of our Lord. It is a mysticism in which *Light* and *Glory* have great part; and the Eastern mind is Biblical enough and simple enough not to shrink from a physical idea of light, since the goal of a transformed creation is that God's children will in literalness *see* Him as He is. Small wonder that such a religion puts August 6th high among the commemorations of the mysteries of Christ:

> Thou wast transfigured upon the mount, O Christ God, revealing unto thy disciples thy glory in so far as they could bear it. Let thy light everlasting illumine us sinners also through the prayers of the birth-giver of God. O light-giver, glory to thee.

The most recent work of Eastern theologians shews that the Transfiguration still holds its traditional place. Sergius Boulgakoff, theologian of the Russian Academy in Paris who died in 1943, beloved of many in England, devoted some pages to the Transfiguration in his *Du Verbe Incarné* (Paris 1943, translated from the Russian by Constantin Anchonikof). He characteristically sees it as a manifestation of glory not only in Christ but also 'in the world, transfigured with Him in some of its parts: the garments, the air around, the mountains and the earth.' The event has its place among those 'semblables accomplissements théanthropiques' in our Lord's ministry which are 'above t me'. Just as the institution of the Eucharist anticipates the Passion which is fore-accomplished in Christ's decision to die, and just as the Prayer in John xvii anticipates the completion of the glorifying, so too the Transfiguration prefigures Calvary and the subsequent glory as things 'already hidden in the decision of the Saviour concerning His departure to Jerusalem to meet there His redeeming Passion'. Further, the event was not only for the edification of the disciples but for Christ Himself: it was 'non seulement comme le témoignage de la gloire, mais comme l'*état* même de celle-ci car le Christ y est déjà illuminé par le gloire'. What the Baptism is to the public ministry of Jesus, the Transfiguration is to the Passion. In both events the Spirit descends. At Jordan the Spirit comes to Him for the fulfilment of His work as *prophet*, on the mountain the Spirit (symbolized by the cloud) comes to Him for His mission as *priest*. There and then He is glorified, for the glory is His acceptance of the path of suffering and Calvary is anticipated in the decision to suffer. Indeed we may see in the Transfiguration the designation of our Lord as priest for ever after the order of Melchizedek, 'who through the eternal Spirit offered himself without blemish unto God' (Heb. ix, 4).

IV—*The Transfiguration in the English Church*

The Reformation added little to the interpretation of the Transfiguration. The shift of emphasis from the Gospels to the Pauline Epistles, the violent reaction from distorted views of the communion of saints, the distrust of mysticism, suffice to explain this neglect. Amid the distortion of the balance and fullness of Christian truth on both sides of the sixteenth-century controversies the Transfiguration made little distinctive appeal, symbolizing as it did some of those unities—Cross and Resurrection, redemption and creation—which mediaeval and post-mediaeval theology in the West often missed.

In England the Transfiguration had been observed locally in early times, and the Bull of Callixtus III had later led to its inclusion in the Sarum Kalendar. But it fared badly at the hands of the Reformers, so badly that it disappeared altogether in the Prayer Book of 1549. It was restored to the Calendar in 1561, and there it remained in the Prayer Book of 1662 but without the provision of Collect, Epistle and Gospel. Hence for nearly three centuries the Church of England has been left with only a Black-letter day to remind her of the Transfiguration. But she has possessed, in the scriptures and in the appeal to antiquity, the power of recovery; and some of her great teachers have not left the Transfiguration out of account.

It is chiefly to the homiletic literature that the student of English thought upon the Transfiguration has to turn. Here the place of honour perhaps belongs still to Joseph Hall's 'Three Contemplations of the Transfiguration' included in his work *The Contemplations*. Bishop successively of Exeter and Norwich, Hall delivered the first two of these 'contemplations' as discourses before King James I and his court. Specially memorable is his consideration of the converse of Moses and Elias concerning the Lord's decease: 'A strange opportunity . . . when his head shone with glory, to tell him how it must bleed with thorns; when his face shone like the sun, to tell him it must be blubbered and spat upon; when his garments glistered with celestial brightness, to tell him they must be stripped and divided . . . and whilst he was Transfigured on the Mount, to tell him how he must be Disfigured on the Cross!' Memorable also is his contrast between the *bonum est hic esse* of the lover of Christ and the *bonum est hic esse* of the worldly courtier, and his comment on Peter's nterjection: 'it was a *praematura devotio* . . . effutuit labiis, he spake inadvisedly with his lips'. 'The cloud imports both Majesty and Obscuration . . . if a light to cheer us, we must have a cloud to humble us.' The voice tells of the divine pleasure which can rest upon Christ alone: 'let me be found in Christ, and how canst thou but be pleased with me.'

In homiletics there has been no lack in England of expositions of the Transfiguration.[1] The careful exegetical treatment of Archbishop Trench in his *Studies in the Gospel* (1867) is still a mine of valuable information. But a distinctively theological treatment is hardly found until Westcott. He, in a few brief references which he makes to the Transfiguration, shews that his conception of its meaning is closely akin to his thought about the Resurrection. 'We see in the risen Christ', he wrote, 'the end for which man was made, and the assurance that the end is in reach. The Resurrection, if we may so speak, shews us the change which would have passed over the earthly life of man, if sin had not brought in death.'[2] Similarly 'the Transfiguration is the revelation of the potential spirituality of the earthly life in the highest outward form. Such an event, distinct in its teaching from the Resurrection, and yet closely akin to it, calls for more religious recognition than it receives. . . . Here the Lord, as Son of Man, gives the measure of the capacity of humanity, and shews that to which He leads those who are united with Him.'[3]

---

[1] These examples have distinction: J. H. Newman: *Parochial and Plain Sermons*, vol. III, xviii; F. D. Maurice: *The Gospel of the Kingdom of Heaven*, ch. XIII; A. S. Farrar (Professor of Divinity in the University of Durham): *Science in Theology*, ch. VI; L. P. Crawfurd: *The Transfiguration, A Manifestation of God in Man*; J. N. Figgis: *Some Defects in English Religion*, ch. X; John Wordsworth: *Sermons and Selected Prayers*, ch. XXIX.
[2] *The Revelation of the Risen Lord*, p. xxxv.
[3] *The Historic Faith*, p. 256.

GLORY AND TRANSFIGURATION

Westcott does not here say in so many words that the Transfiguration indicates the proper destiny of the Son of Man if it had not been the divine will that He should identify Himself with sinful humanity by dying. The nearest approach that he makes to this conception is in a note on Hebrews ii, 15, where he says: 'The passage from one form of life to another, which is involved in the essential transitoriness of man's constitution, might have been joyful. As it is, death brings to our apprehension the sense of an unnatural break in personal being, and of separation from God. This pain comes from sin.' Further than this Westcott does not go. But other English theologians, building on the logic of the connection of sin and death and on the idea of the deathlessness of a sinless humanity, have written of the Transfiguration as the offer to Jesus of a painless and deathless ascent to His destiny, instead of which ascent He willed to fulfil His exodus by dying in Jerusalem.[1] It seems indeed true to assert that the Transfiguration is a glimpse of Man's proper destiny. But it seems precarious to assert that the possibility of a departure without death there and then lay before our Lord, for perhaps the Incarnation itself had already meant the entrance by the Son of God into a manhood lived under all the conditions of the sphere in which sin reigned.

Westcott's conception of the Transfiguration as the revelation of 'the measure of the capacity of humanity' lends itself to expansion and development in connection with an organic view of the world. In a striking article in *Theology*, April 1931, E. L. Mascall discussed the relation of the Incarnation to a philosophy of organism, and in the course of the discussion made an interesting reference to the Transfiguration. 'Just as, in the body of a living creature, there is no abrupt violation of the laws of physics, but rather those laws are absorbed as ingredients into the wider laws of physiology, so in Christ the perfect development from infancy to manhood does not destroy His humanity, but elicits its true function by rendering it the perfect organ of His divine self-expression to the Universe. The reality of this development is shewn by the Transfiguration. In the transfigured Christ the system of relations which forms His humanity no

---

[1] Cf. W. J. Sparrow-Simpson: *Our Lord's Resurrection*, pp. 216-23; F. S. M. Bennett: *The Resurrection of the Dead*, pp. 156-61.

THE TRANSFIGURATION IN THE CHURCH

longer manifests it as subject to the normal laws of science, but shews it to be governed by new laws into which the old have been absorbed by a process of continuous modification. . . .'
Mascall would not claim that this conception is to be derived from the event of the Transfiguration, but that an organic view of the Incarnation and the world, with the Resurrection as its climax, suggests an interpretation of the Transfiguration congruous with the whole incarnational process. The event is specially congruous with the aspect of the Incarnation described in the words 'one, not by the conversion of the Godhead into flesh, but by the taking of the manhood into God'.

The revival however of a richer *Lex Credendi* is linked with the recovery of the *Lex Orandi*, and this has been a notable feature of modern Anglicanism in relation to the Transfiguration. Honour is due to the Episcopal Church of the United States of America which made the Transfiguration a Red-letter Day in 1886. The Scottish Church, the Church of South Africa and the Canadian Church have revived the observance in like manner; and its inclusion in the Deposited Book of 1928 has made its recognition familiar in many English parishes, where Christian people pray that God who before the Passion of His Son revealed His glory upon the holy mount, may grant to them that they may be strengthened to bear the Cross and be changed into His likeness from glory to glory.

CHAPTER XIV

THE GOSPEL OF TRANSFIGURATION

1

THE TRANSFIGURATION does not belong to the central core of the Gospel. The apostolic *Kerygma* did not, so far as we know, include it; and it would be hard for Christians to claim that the salvation of mankind could not be wrought without it. But it stands as a gateway to the saving events of the Gospel, and is as a mirror in which the Christian mystery is seen in its unity. Here we perceive that the living and the dead are one in Christ, that the old covenant and the new are inseparable, that the Cross and the glory are of one, that the age to come is already here, that our human nature has a destiny of glory, that in Christ the final word is uttered and in Him alone the Father is well pleased. Here the diverse elements in the theology of the New Testament meet.

Forgetfulness of the truths for which the Transfiguration stands has often led to distortions. The severance of the New Testament from the Old, the cleavage between God the Redeemer and God the Creator are obvious illustrations. It is possible, alike in Christology and in sacramental teaching and in the idea of the Christian life, to regard the supernatural as replacing the natural in such a way as to 'overthrow the nature of a sacrament'. It is possible to regard the redemptive act of God in Christ in terms so transcendental that nature and history are not seen in real relation to it, or to identify the divine act with nature and history in such a way that the other-worldly tension of the Gospel is forgotten. Against these distortions the Transfiguration casts its light in protest.

2

'The Transfiguration', wrote F. D. Maurice, 'has lived on through ages, and shed its light upon all ages. . . . In the light of

THE GOSPEL OF TRANSFIGURATION

that countenance which was altered, of that raiment which was white and glistering, all human countenances have acquired a brightness, all common things have been transfigured.'[1] So great is the impact of theology upon language that the word 'transfigure', drawn from a Biblical story to which scant attention has often been paid, has entered into the practical vocabulary of the Christian life.

1. To the Christian suffering is transfigured. 'Our tribulation without ceasing to be tribulation is transformed. We must suffer, as we suffered before, but our suffering is no longer a passive perplexity . . . but is transformed into a pain which is fruitful, creative, full of power and promise. . . . The road which is impassable has been made known to us in the crucified and risen Lord.'[2]

2. To the Christian knowledge is transfigured. The knowledge of the world and its forces may be used for the service of man's pride and man's destruction, or else for the unfolding of God's truth and the enlarging of God's worship. 'It is not too much to say', wrote Dr. Hort, 'that the Gospel itself can never be fully known till nature as well as man is fully known; and that the manifestation of nature as well as man in Christ is part of His manifestation of God. As the Gospel is the perfect introduction to all truth, so on the other hand it is in itself known only in proportion as it is used for the enlightenment of departments of truth which seem at first sight to lie beyond its boundaries. . . . The earth as well as the heaven is full of God's glory, and His visible glory is but the garment of His truth, so that every addition to truth becomes a fresh opportunity for adoration.'[3]

3. To the Christian the world is transfigured. Liberated from its dominance he discovers it afresh as the scene both of divine judgment and of divine renewal within the new creation of Christ. The measure in which he accepts the judgment is the measure in which he discerns, in the face of every calamity, the divine renewal in the raising of the dead.

The transfiguring of pain, of knowledge and of the world is

[1] *The Gospel of the Kingdom of Heaven*, p. 157.
[2] Karl Barth: *The Epistle to the Romans*, English translation (Oxford Press), p. 156.
[3] F. J. A. Hort: *The Way, The Truth, The Life*, pp. 83-4.

GLORY AND TRANSFIGURATION

attested in centuries of the experience of Christians. It comes neither by an acceptance of things as they are nor by a flight from them, but by that uniquely Christian attitude which the story of the Transfiguration represents. It is an attitude which is rooted in detachment—for pain is hateful, knowledge is corrupted and the world lies in the evil one, but which so practises detachment as to return and perceive the divine sovereignty in the very things from which the detachment has had to be. Thus the Christian life is a rhythm of going and coming; and the gospel narrative of the ascent of Hermon, the metamorphosis and the descent to a faithless and perverse generation is a symbol of the mission of the Church in its relation to the world.

3

Our contemporary distresses have not made the message of Mount Hermon obsolete. Analysing the possibilities open to those who are aware that they live in a 'declining civilization' Dr. Toynbee distinguishes four principles: archaism, futurism, detachment, transfiguration. *Archaism* is the yearning for a past golden age; *futurism* is a phantasy of a new age utterly unrelated to that which now exists, and the quest of it is often pursued by violent means; *detachment* (for which 'escapism' would be a better word, since Christians know detachment in a good sense) is an escape into contemplation; but *transfiguration* is a faith whereby 'we bring the total situation, as we ourselves participate in it, into a larger context which gives it a new meaning.'[1] Of such a faith, so the contention of this book has been, the Biblical doctrine of the GLORY provides the pattern and the event of the Transfiguration provides the symbol. Peter on Mount Hermon may have longed to *return* to the happiness of his discipleship before the Passion was announced, or to *escape* from the conflict into a heavenly rest, or to *advance* at once into the peace of the last things. But the Transfiguration meant the taking of the whole conflict of the Lord's mission, just as it was, into the glory which gave meaning to it all.

[1] The phrase is C. H. Dodd's, paraphrasing Toynbee's argument, in *The Bible Today*, p. 129. Toynbee's thesis may be found in his *A Study of History* (Abridged Volume) pp. 221 ff, 435 ff, 528 ff.

THE GOSPEL OF TRANSFIGURATION

Confronted as he is with a universe more than ever terrible in the blindness of its processes and the destructiveness of its potentialities mankind must be led to the Christian faith not as a panacea of progress nor as an other-worldly solution unrelated to history, but as a Gospel of Transfiguration. Such a Gospel both transcends the world and speaks to the immediate here-and-now. He who is transfigured is the Son of Man; and, as He discloses on mount Hermon another world, He reveals that no part of created things and no moment of created time lies outside the power of the Spirit, who is Lord, to change from glory into glory.

APPENDIX I

JESUS CHRIST: THE GLORY AND THE IMAGE

I

IT WILL be apparent from the first part of this book how close is the connection between the glory of God and the person of Jesus Christ in the New Testament writings. In three kinds of passage the connection is particularly shewn. (1) There are passages where the glory of God is so manifested through Jesus Christ that the content of the glory is characterized by that manifestation. Amongst many instances John i, 14 and 2 Cor, iv, 6 may be cited. (2) There are passages where glory is mentioned as an attribute of Christ Himself, and the context in each case shews that Christ's glory and God's glory can hardly be separated. These passages are Luke ix, 26 ('when he cometh in his own glory and the glory of the Father and of the holy angels': contrast Mark viii, 38 where 'his own glory' is absent), Luke ix, 32; xxiv, 26; John ii, 11; xvii, 24; 2 Cor. iv, 4. (3) There are passages which go further and seem to contain an identification of Christ with the glory or Shekinah. It is not certain that this identification occurs in *all* the passages where scholars have suggested its presence, and the possible instances call for examination.

1. Eph. i, 17: 'that the God of our Lord Jesus Christ, the Father of the glory, may give unto you a spirit of wisdom and revelation in the knowledge of him.' Here 'the glory' may be a title for Christ, but it would be not unnatural for the genitive to be used adjectively in relation to the Father—'the glorious Father', 'the Father whose characteristic is glory'.

2. Col. i, 27: 'to whom god was pleased to make known what is the riches of the glory of this mystery among the Gentiles, which is Christ in you the hope of glory.' Here the glory, no less than the mystery, may be equivalent to 'Christ in you'. But

APPENDICES

parallels in Rom. ix, 23; Eph. i, 18, iii, 16 support Lightfoot's translation: 'the wealth of the glorious manifestation.'

3. James ii, 1 is a more likely instance of the identification. R.V. reads: 'My brethren, hold not the faith of our Lord Jesus Christ, *the Lord* of glory, with respect of persons.' But this is not an obvious translation of τοῦ Κυρίου ἡμῶν Ιησου Χριστοῦ τῆς δόξης since it severely strains the order of the words (for 'Lord of glory', cf. 1 Cor. ii, 8, and nine times in the Book of Enoch). The Peshitto and the Vulgate connect τῆς δόξης with 'the faith', i.e. 'faith in the glory of our Lord Jesus Christ'. Erasmus and Calvin connect τῆς δόξης with 'respect of persons', taking δόξα to mean 'opinion'. But the order of the words would seem to exclude both these interpretations, and to demand that τῆς δόξης be connected with 'our Lord Jesus Christ'. But how? Suggestions have been 'the Messiah of glory', but this would need the article before Χριστοῦ; 'our Lord of glory Jesus Christ', but why then the order of words which we have? 'our glorious Lord Jesus Christ', but would a genitive of quality be attached to a phrase complete in itself? None of these suggestions seems preferable to the R.V. Rejecting all these suggestions Mayor urged that the proper translation is 'our Lord Jesus Christ, the glory': Christ is Himself the Shekinah in the midst of the congregation, and they must not confound their faith in His presence among them with snobbish thoughts and actions. This interpretation makes good sense, and it fits the Greek better than the others.

4. 1 Peter iv, 14 reads in R.V.: 'the spirit of glory and the spirit of God resteth upon you'. But this translation seems somewhat forced out of τὸ τῆς δόξης καὶ τὸ τοῦ Θεοῦ πνεῦμα. Clearly there is a reminiscence of Isaiah xi, 2 (LXX), the spirit of the Lord resting upon the Messiah; but the relation between the spirit and τὸ τῆς δόξης is a little obscure. Selwyn suggests that the idiom τὸ τῆς means 'the presence of', and compares 1 Sam. vi, 4 (LXX) and Matt. xxi, 21, τὸ τῆς συκῆς: 'what rests upon the church is not quite the glory, but the communicable part or presence, which he goes on to explain as the Spirit of God.' This virtually identifies τὸ τῆς δόξης with the Shekinah; but it does not involve *equating* the Shekinah with Jesus Christ, as is involved by a translation 'the Spirit of the glory' (i.e. Jesus Christ) and of God'. The passage, as Selwyn interprets it, is in

GLORY AND TRANSFIGURATION

keeping with the N.T. teaching in which both glory and spirit anticipate the eschatological goal of the Christian life, and in which glory and suffering are linked: cf. 2 Cor. iii, 7 and xii, 9.

5. John i, 14: 'the word was made flesh and dwelt among us, and we beheld his glory.' The close connection here between the Incarnate Son and the δόξα and σκηνή hardly falls short of an identification between them.

In spite therefore of the uncertainty of the meaning of some of the relevant passages there seems to be good evidence that the early Church thought of Jesus as Himself the manifestation of the glory of God. A parallel in rabbinic literature may be seen in the comment of Simeon ben Jochai on Ps. ii, where he speaks of 'The Lord of the serving angels, the son of the Highest, yea, the Shekinah.' And in Justin Martyr, *Dialogue against Trypho*, 61, we read: 'God begat from Himself a certain immaterial Dynamis, which is called the glory of the Lord, and sometimes the Son, and sometimes the Wisdom.'

2

The statement in 1 Cor. xi, 7 that 'man is the image and glory of God' links the doctrine of the δόξα to the doctrine of the εἰκών. The latter word is used in the New Testament both of the divine image in which the human race was created, and of the image of Christ into which redeemed humanity is transformed. Hence its use provides an important reminder of the unity of the doctrines of creation and redemption.

1. *Christ is the image of God*, Col. i, 15, 2 Cor. iv, 4. The word εἰκών means 'that which resembles' (ἔοικα), and in particular the resemblance of something to a prototype from which it is derived and in whose essence it shares. Christ is 'the image of the invisible god' (Col. i, 15) in that He shares in God's real being and hence can be a perfect manifestation of that being. Kittel comments: 'Even if it were not accompanied by the words "Son of his love" it is clear that the image-figure is only an attempt to speak in another way of His relation as Son.' (*Theologisches Wörterbuch* ii, p. 394.)

2. *Man is created in the image of God*, 1 Cor. xi, 7. This doctrine goes back to Genesis i, 26. We are prevented from

APPENDICES

drawing wrong inferences from this doctrine by the recollection of the recurring insistence of Scripture upon the distinction between man as creature and God as Creator: while Christ is the uncreated image of deity, man is *created* in the image of God. As such he possesses a true affinity to his Creator, an affinity whereon the possibility of his redemption and knowledge of God rest. The image in man is defaced by sin, bringing the frustration or vanity which only the grace of God can cure. But man is not totally depraved (cf. Rom. i, 20; ii, 15); and man, when he is raised up with Christ in glory, will be man as God created him to become—both in his likeness to his Maker and in his utter dependence upon Him.

3. *Man is transformed into the image of Christ*, so as to become like unto Christ's perfect manhood, 1 Cor. xv, 49; 2 Cor. iii, 18; Rom. viii, 28; Col. iii, 9–10. In Christ mankind is allowed to see not only the radiance of God's glory but also the true image of man. Into that image Christ's people are now being transformed, and in virtue of this transformation into the new man they are realizing the meaning of their original status as creatures in God's image.[1]

Thus redemption is wrought not *in vacuo* but on the groundwork of creation. Through the work of Christ man becomes what man essentially is. 'Werde das du bist' summarizes the Biblical doctrine. In Christ there is our human nature fulfilling both its true affinity to the creator and its true dependence upon Him in adoration; and the more we are brought to share in Christ's glory the more shall we share in that giving glory to the Father which was His mission and is our calling.

[1] Cf. Kittel's comment on Col. iii, 9–10: 'die Wiedergewinnung der schöpfungsmäszigen Gottes-Ebenbildlichkeit ist identisch mit der Herstellung der Christusgemeinschaft', op. cit., p. 395.

APPENDIX II

SOME ENGLISH COLLECTS

It may be of interest to give the text of some collects which present to English Churchmen the many-sided doctrine which the Transfiguration embodies. The American Prayer Book has this:

> O God, who on the mount didst reveal to chosen witnesses thine only-begotten Son wonderfully transfigured in raiment white and glistering, mercifully grant that we being delivered from the disquietude of this world may be permitted to behold the King in His Beauty.

The Scottish Prayer Book has this:

> Almighty and everlasting God, whose blessed Son revealed himself to his chosen apostles when he was transfigured on the holy mount, and amidst the excellent glory spake with Moses and Elijah of his decease which he should accomplish at Jerusalem: grant to us thy servants that, beholding the brightness of thy countenance, we may be strengthened to bear the Cross.

The one flaw in this admirable collect is its reference to the face of the Father, where a reference to the face of the Son would seem far more appropriate. The latter is accordingly mentioned in the Collect in the English Deposited Book of 1927–1928.

> O God, who before the passion of thine only-begotten Son didst reveal his glory upon the holy mount: grant unto us thy servants that in faith beholding the light of his countenance we may be strengthened to bear the Cross, and be changed into his likeness from glory to glory.

Bishop John Wordsworth in *The Ministry of Grace* (second edition, p. 422) wrote: 'I have sometimes used a version of another Latin collect', and provided the version which seems to be based neither upon the Roman or the Sarum Missal.

APPENDICES

O God, who didst call the saints of the old covenant to bear witness to thy Son's Transfiguration, and by a voice from the cloud of light didst bid us hearken unto Him: grant that as we have found Him in deed the only perfect teacher of the truth, so we may one day behold Him face to face in glory.

For the Roman and Sarum Collects see p. 129 of this book. An English office of the Transfiguration is provided by Dr. L. B. Radford, late Bishop of Goulburn, in *The Transfiguration of our Lord* (Faith Press, 1937).

SELECT BIBLIOGRAPHY

I—The Glory of God

ABRAHAMS, I.: *The Glory of God*, 1925.
VON GALL, A.: *Die Herrlichkeit Gottes*, 1900.
GRAY, G. B.: Article on 'Glory' in *Hastings' Dictionary of the Bible*.
HOSKYNS, E. C.: *The Fourth Gospel*, 1940.
KENNEDY, H. A. A.: *Saint Paul's Conception of the Last Things*, 1904.
KITTEL, GERHARD: Article on '$\Delta \acute{o} \xi a$' in *Theologisches Wörterbuch zum Neuentestament*, 1934.
KITTEL, HELMUD: *Die Herrlichkeit Gottes, Studien zu Geschichte und Wesen eines nt. lichen Begriffes*, 1935.
VON HÜGEL, F.: *Essays and Addresses*, 1928.
HODGSON, L.: *The Doctrine of the Trinity*, 1943.
MARSHALL, R. T.: Article on 'Shekinah' in *Hastings' Dictionary of the Bible*.
MIDDLETON, R. D.: 'Logos and Shekinah in the Fourth Gospel' in *Jewish Quarterly Review*, Oct. 1938.
MOORE, G. F.: 'Intermediaries in Jewish Theology' in *Harvard Theological Review*, Jan. 1922.
SELWYN, E. G.: *The First Epistle of Saint Peter*, 1946.
THORNTON, L. S.: *The Common Life in the Body of Christ*, 1943.
UNDERHILL, E.: *Worship*, 1936.

II—The Transfiguration in the New Testament

BADCOCK, F. J.: 'The Transfiguration' in *Journal of Theological Studies*, July 1921.
BARRY, G. D.: *The Transfiguration of Christ*, 1911.
BOOBYER, G.: *Saint Mark and the Transfiguration Story*, 1942.

BIBLIOGRAPHY

BERNARDIN, J. B.: 'The Transfiguration' in *Journal of Biblical Literature*, 1933.
HARNACK, A.: 'Die Verklärungsgeschichte Jesu' in *Sitzungsberichte der Preussichen Akademie der Wissenschaft*, 1922.
KENNEDY, H. A. A.: 'The Purpose of the Transfiguration' in *Journal of Theological Studies*, Jan. 1903.
HOLMES, R.: 'The Purpose of the Transfiguration' in *Journal of Theological Studies*, July 1903.
LOHMEYER, E.: 'Die Verklärung Jesu nach dem Markus Evangelium' in *Zeitschrift für Neutestamentliche Wissenschaft*, 1922. *Das Evangelium d. Markus*, 1937.
RADFORD, L. B., Bishop of Goulburn: *The Transfiguration of our Lord*, 1937.
RIESENFELD, H.: *Jésus Transfiguré*, 1947.
SPENS, MAISIE: *Concerning Himself*, 1938.
TRENCH, R. C.: *Studies in the Gospels*, fifth edn. 1886.
UNDERHILL, E.: *The Mystic Way*, 1913.
ANONYMOUS: 'The Baptism, Temptation and Transfiguration: a Study' in *Church Quarterly Review*, July 1901.

III—*The Transfiguration in Worship and Doctrine*

ARSENIEV, N.: *Mysticism and the Eastern Church*, 1924.
BOULGAKOV, S.: *Du Verbe Incarné*, 1943.
CONYBEARE, F. C.: Valparet: 'The Revelation of our Lord to Peter' in *Z.N.T.W.*, 1921.
CRAWFURD, L. P.: *The Transfiguration, a Manifestation of God in Man*, 1912.
DOWDEN, J.: *The Church Year and Calendar*, 1910.
HAPGOOD, L.: *Service Book of the Eastern Orthodox Church*, 1922.
HALL, JOSEPH: *Contemplations*, new edition 1837.
LEO THE GREAT: Sermon LI in *Nicene and Post Nicene Fathers*, Vol. XII, 1895.
MAURICE, F. D.: *The Gospel of the Kingdom of Heaven*, 1879.
MASCALL, E. L.: 'The Nature of the Resurrection' in *Theology*, May 1931.
WESTCOTT, B. F.: *The Historic Faith*, third edn. 1885.
ANONYMOUS: *Eastern Orthodox Spirituality*, S.P.C.K. 1945.

INDEX OF AUTHORS

Abrahams, I., 9, 11, 154
Ambrose, St., 132
Anselm, St., 119, 131
Arseniev, N., 138, 155
Augustine, St., 71, 130, 131

Badcock, F. J., 154
Barrett, C. K., 52
Barry, G. D., 154
Barth, Karl, 145
Basil, St., 131
Batiffol, P., 129
Bede, Ven., 132
Bengel, 68, 88, 123
Bennett, F. S. M., 142
Bernard, J. H., 78
Bernardin, J. B., 155
Boobyer, G. H., 103, 106, 109–10, 118, 154
Boulgakov, S., 139–40, 154
Brooke, A. E., 53
Bruce, A. B., 44
Bultmann, R., 104
Burney, C. F., 58–9

Callixtus, Nicephorus, 128
Clement of Alexandria, 132
Conybeare, F. C., 135, 155
Crawford, L. P., 141, 155

Dodd, C. H., 146
Dowden, J., 155
Driver, S. R., 9

Ebner, 129
Eichrodt, W., 10

Farrar, A. S., 141

Figgis, J. N., 141
Forsyth, P. T., 85

Gall, F. von, 10, 54, 154
Goetz, K., 106
Goudge, H. L., 100
Gray, G. B., 10, 13, 154
Gregory of Nyssa, 12, 85
Gregory, Pope, 131

Hall, Bishop, 140, 155
Hapgood, L., 155
Harnack, A. von, 117, 155
Hodgson, L., 83, 84, 154
Holmes, R., 155
Holmes, W. H. G., 44
Hort, F. J. A., 52, 73, 145
Hoskyns, E. C., 73, 124, 154
Hügel, F. von, 154

Jeremias, J., 114
Jerome, St., 131
Justin Martyr, 150

Kennedy, H. A. A., 48, 154, 155
Kittel, Gerhard, 23, 53, 55, 118, 150, 151, 154
Kittel, Helmud, 11, 24, 39, 47, 154
Klostermann, E., 114
Knox, W. L., 25, 53, 60, 76

Lagrange, M. J., 70
Latham, H., 117
Leo, Pope, 129, 131, 133–5, 155
Lietzmann, H., 27
Lohmeyer, E., 102, 110–11, 116, 155
Loisy, A., 70, 75, 104, 105, 123
Lowther-Clark, W. K., 30, 108

INDEX

Manson, W., 38
Marshall, R. T., 154
Mascall, E. L., 83, 142-3, 155
Masure, E., 84
Maurice, F. D., 64, 141, 144, 155
Mayor, J. B., 149
Meyer, E., 117
Middleton, R. D., 19, 154
Milligan, G., 34
Moffatt, J., 124-6
Montefiore, G. C., 20, 104
Moore, G. F., 19, 154
Mowinckel, 14, 15, 103

Newman, J. H., 141

Origen, 130-1

Pedersen, J., 9
Plummer, A., 112

Rad, von, 10, 17
Radford, L. B., 153, 155

Riesenfeld, 103-4, 118
Rowley, H. H., 15

Schlatter, A., 48, 54, 60, 115, 116
Selwyn, E. G., 27, 41, 42, 149, 154
Skinner, J., 17
Spens, Maisie, 107-8, 155
Strachan, R. H., 64

Tertullian, 130
Theodoret, 131
Thornton, L. S., 91, 124, 154
Toynbee, A., 146
Trench, R. C., 112, 141, 155
Tristram, H., 113

Underhill, E., 86, 106-7, 154, 155

Wellhausen, J., 104, 105
Westcott, B. F., 44, 62, 71, 76, 141, 155
Wordsworth, John, 141, 152

INDEX OF SUBJECTS

Acts of Apostles, 31, 95
Apocalypse of Peter, 105-6
Apocalyptic writers, 20-1, 29, 31, 32-3, 109-10
Atonement, 76, 86-7, 150-1, and passim

Baptism, 55

Church, 70, 72-81, 87-9, 95-100
Cloud, 11-12, 16-19, 21, 109, 115, 120, 122, 132, 139, 141
Creation, 28, 46, 83, 96, 138, 150-1

Eastern Church, 135-40
Enoch, Book of, 20-1
ἐπισκιάζειν, 39, 115
Eschatology, 28, 29-35, 50-6, 89-90, 117-18, 131

Eucharist, 75-80, 98-9, 137, 139

Father, The, 31, 49, 64, 65, 72-5, 83-4, 148
Fathers of the Church, 130-6
Festival of Transfiguration, 128-9, 143, 152-3

Gospel, The, 36-8, 47-8, 99-100, 144-7
Gospels:
 Matthew, 29-30, 36-8, 95, 112, 120
 Mark, 29-30, 36-8, 102-3, 112-19
 Luke, 36-40, 93-95, 112, 121-123
 John, 40, 44, 57-81, 84-87, 123-4

Hebrews, Epistle to, 43-5, 94, 126, 142

INDEX

Holy Spirit, 33, 51–2, 55–6, 74–5, 81, 87, 132, 139, 149

Image, 53–4, 150–1
Incarnation, 57–62, 84–6
Isaiah, 13–14, 25, 59

James, Epistle of, 149
Judgment, 67–8, 100
Justification, 47, 54

Kingdom, 30, 36–8, 132

Light, 11, 14, 21, 23, 32–3, 34, 39, 47–8, 50, 83, 106, 109, 120, 126, 136–9, 152

Marcion, 126, 130
Moses, 12, 17, 120
Moses and Elijah, 19, 107–10, 114, 130–4, 136

Parousia, 29–30, 34, 41–2, 55–6, 103, 109, 118, 131–2

Passion, 38, 40–5, 65–8, 69–81, 86–7, 94, 116, 121–3, 133, 139–40
Peter, First Epistle of, 32–3, 41–2, 127
Peter, Second Epistle of, 124–6
Psalms, 12, 14–15, 92, 97–8
Paul, Conversion of, 32, 48
Power, 11, 13, 30–1, 49, 82

Resurrection, 31–2, 40, 50, 55, 66, 81, 117, 135–7, 141–3
Riches, 9, 27, 49

Septuagint, 23–6, 59, 111
Servant of the Lord, 25, 41, 68
Shekinah, 19–20, 24, 28, 58–60, 148–50
Signs of Jesus, 62–5
Storm-theophany, 10–11

Tabernacle, 16–17, 25–6, 58–60, 110–11, 115, 118
Temple, 17–18, 60, 73, 88
Trinity, The Holy, 75, 84, 131–2

INDEX OF PRINCIPAL PASSAGES IN SCRIPTURE

OLD TESTAMENT

Genesis xxxi, 1	9	Psalms xvi, 9	9	
xlix, 6	9	xix, 1	83	
Exodus xiv, 19–24	16	xxix, 3–5	11	
xv, 11	25	lvii, 11	15	
xxiv, 16–17	17	lxxxv, 9–10	15, 25, 38, 61	
xxxiii, 9–10	16	xcvi, 3	15	
xxxiii, 12–23	12, 25	xcvii, 2–6	12	
xl, 35	39	cxlv, 11	30, 92	
Numbers xiv, 22	12	Proverbs xviii, 11	39	
xxxv, 34	25	Isaiah vi, 1–4	13, 59	
Deuteronomy v, 24	12	xxxv, 1–6	37	
xviii, 15	114	xl, 4–5	14, 37	
xxxiv, 10	114	lii, 13–liii	25, 41, 68	
1 Kings viii, 10–12	17	lx, 1–3	14	
2 Chronicles vii, 1–3	17	Jeremiah xxiii, 23	22	
		Ezekiel 1, 28	16	
		ix, 3	16	

INDEX

Ezekiel x, 18–24	16	John xiii	69–72
xi, 22	16	xiv–xvi	72–5
xxviii, 22	92	xvii	67, 70, 72, 75–80, 87, 98–9
xxxix, 13	92		
xliii, 1–5	16	xviii–xx	81
Zechariah ii, 9–10	19, 25	xxi, 19	96
xiv, 16–19	111	Acts iii, 13	31
Malachi iv, 5–6	110	vii, 55	31
		iv, 21	95
		xi, 18	95
APOCRYPHA		xiii, 48	95
		xxi, 20	95
2 Esdras (4 Ezra) vi, 26	109	Romans i, 17	54
vii, 78	21	i, 20, 23	46
Tobit xiii, 10	111	iii, 23–4	47
Ecclesiasticus xliv, 1–2	26	v, 1–2	32, 47, 50
2 Maccabees ii, 7	21, 115	vi, 4	31
		viii, 18	32, 50, 90
		viii, 21	90
NEW TESTAMENT		viii, 30	47, 87
		xi, 33–6	96
Matthew xvi, 28	132	xv, 6, 9	96
xvii, 1–9	112, 120	xvi, 25–7	96
xix, 28	30	1 Corinthians ii, 8	84
xx, 21	30	iii, 16–17	88
xxv, 31	29	vi, 20	96
Mark i, 15	36	x, 31	96
ii, 12	95	xi, 7	27, 150
viii, 38	29	xiii, 12	53, 90
ix, 1	132	2 Corinthians iii, 7–11	51, 150
ix, 2–9	113–19	iii, 9	47
x, 37	30	iii, 11	120
xiii, 26	29	iii, 12–18	52–4, 87, 99, 114, 127, 151
Luke ii, 9, 14, 30–2	39		
ix, 26	40, 148		
ix, 28–36	39, 40, 121–3, 133, 148	iv, 3–6	47, 49, 148, 150
xix, 37–8	40, 95	iv, 18	55
xxiii, 47	95	vi, 16	88
xxiv, 26	40, 148	ix, 13	96
John i, 14	57–62, 84, 150	xii, 9	150
i, 18	61, 116	Galatians i, 4–5	96
ii–x	62–5	i, 24	95
ii, 11	63, 148	vi, 14	41
v, 44	27, 65, 68	Ephesians i, 5–6	49, 96
xi–xii	66–8	i, 17	49, 148
xii, 27–30	67, 71, 124	i, 18	27, 49

INDEX

Ephesians ii, 21-2	88	Hebrews ii, 9-10	44, 90
iii, 20-1	96	xiii, 20-1	96
v, 8	32	James ii, 1	149
Philippians i, 11	96	1 Peter i, 21	31
iii, 21	32, 90	ii, 4-5	88
Colossians i, 11	49	iv, 13	32, 41
i, 12	32	iv, 14	33, 42, 149
i, 15	150	iv, 16	96
i, 27	148	v, 1	42, 127
iii, 1-4	55, 88	v, 10	41
iii, 4	34, 50	2 Peter i, 16-21	125
iii, 9-10	151	1 John iii, 2	62, 80, 90, 127
1 Thessalonians ii, 12	30	Jude 24-5	96
2 Thessalonians iii, 1	96	Revelation i, 6	97
1 Timothy i, 17	96	v, 13	97
iii, 16	31, 34	xv, 4	97
2 Timothy iv, 18	96	xiv, 6-7	100
Titus ii, 13	32, 34	xviii, 1	39
Hebrews i, 3	43	xxi, 1-3	118